¡Tequila!

¡Tequila!

A Natural and Cultural History

▲ ▲ ▲ ▲ ▲ ▲ ▲ ▲ ▲ ▲

ANA GUADALUPE VALENZUELA-ZAPATA

AND

GARY PAUL NABHAN

The University of Arizona Press   Tucson

The University of Arizona Press
© 2003 Ana Guadalupe Valenzuela-Zapata and Gary Paul Nabhan

Third Printing

www.uapress.arizona.edu

Library of Congress Cataloging-in-Publication Data
Valenzuela-Zapata, Ana Guadalupe, 1963–
[El agave tequilero, English]
Tequila : a natural cultural history / Ana Guadalupe Valenzuela-Zapata and Gary
Paul Nabhan.
p. cm.
Includes bibliographical references (p.).
ISBN-10: 0-8165-1937-4 (cloth : alk. paper) —
ISBN-10: 0-8165-1938-2 (pbk. : alk. paper) —
ISBN-13: 978-0-8165-1938-5 (pbk. : alk. paper)
1. Tequila agave—Mexico—Jalisco. 2. Tequila industry—Mexico.
I. Nabhan, Gary Paul. II. Title.
SB317T48 V3413 2004
584'.352—dc21
2003011691

Manufactured in the United States of America on acid-free, archival-quality paper.

22 21 20 19 18 17   8 7 6 5 4 3

Contents

List of Illustrations   vii

Preface: A Handful of Dreams Opened up to the Sun, by Ana
   Guadalupe Valenzuela-Zapata   ix

Acknowledgments   xix

Introduction: Tequila Hangovers and the Mescal Monoculture
   Blues, by Gary Paul Nabhan   xxi

1   Distilling the Essences, Blending Two Worlds   3

2   Mescal de Tequila: The Mexican-American Microcosmos   13

3   The Wild Origins and Domestication of Mescal de Tequila   21

4   Tillers and Tale-Tellers: The Agrarian Tradition of Jimadores   31

5   Out of the Fields, into the Fire: Tradition and Globalization   45

6   When the Epidemic Hit the King of Clones   55

7   Landscape and Pueblo: Putting Tequila in Place   63

8   Dreaming the Future of Tequila   73

Appendix 1. A Mescalero's Lexicon   83

Appendix 2. Common Names for Mescal-Producing Agaves in
   Spanish Dialects and Indigenous Languages Spoken in "Mega-
   Mexico"   91

Appendix 3. Agave Species Domesticated Prehistorically for Food,
   Fiber, Hedge, or Beverage Uses by Indigenous Communities   93

Appendix 4. Species Description of Cultivated Agave Species Historically Used in the Tequila Industry   95

Literature Cited   109

Illustrations

following page 54
Amatitán Valley of Jalisco
Planting vegetative offshoots
Agave intercropping
Cultivar propagation by transplanting bulbils
Flowering agaves
Jimador trimming an agave
Final preparation of the cabeza or piña
Mature agave heads
Steam oven for baking agaves
Baked cabezas on conveyor belts
Fermentation tanks
Distiller measuring alcohol and methanol content
Tequila reposado in oak barrels
Stainless steel vats
Agave heads ready for distillation

in appendix 4
Agave angustifolia ssp. *tequilana* cv. *azul*
Agave angustifolia ssp. *tequilana* cv. *sigüín*
Agave angustifolia cv. *gentryii*
Agave vivipara var. *bermejo*
Agave americana cv. *subtilis*

A Handful of Dreams Opened up to the Sun

Ana Guadalupe Valenzuela-Zapata

▲ ▲ ▲

The hours and years passed as I scrambled around the hills surrounding my home overlooking Guadalajara. I followed water wherever it ran, down rain-fed furrows, arroyos, and small canyons. They were the perfect places for our escapes and explorations. By us, I mean me and the neighboring children, for all of us desired to encounter novel places, plants, and animals. We would meander down into the milpa fields, then follow rivulets flowing full with the summer rains, tracing their courses until we were weary.

When we finally headed home, it would dawn on us that we were to receive another bawling-out from our parents, for they had already pronounced our truancy and tardiness to be habitual. No matter how much we cringed when they scolded us, we never once feared the act of exploration itself. We believed in the freedom it offered us, and knew that all true explorers were driven by the same curiosity that engaged us.

Today, as I look back on these sojourns into the plant world, I realize that such visceral contact with nature remains among the richest pleasures of my life. The countryside always unveils a new handful of surprises with the coming of each season. As the weather changes, rising humidity awakens the slumbering citizens of the soil. Fireflies, those apparitions of the evening, mysteriously flash their lights on, then off again. Armies of ants labor long hours, alerting us to the oncoming thunderstorms. The bloom of bugs we call *mayates* had a way of proliferating in our midst, teaching us to anticipate the rhythm of the rainy season. These players in the literature of nature became inscribed in our hearts and in our imaginations. Once we learned their cadence, we could simply close our eyes and find ourselves running for shelter in a lightning shower, bursting with laughter when we finally reached a refuge, realizing how soaked and disheveled we looked.

The Bones of Mayahuel, the Goddess of Agaves

I had just turned fifteen when the next stretch of the naturalist's path appeared before me. I had not been seeking it; it simply opened up on its own, a sudden gift that sent me on an unanticipated trajectory.

The gift came in the form of a plant, lovely and enigmatic, although already a bit tattered. Its leaves were somewhat limp, as if the plant had recently wilted, perhaps in the effort to put out flowers. The flowers themselves were withered and tinged with mold. The plant's vigor had been spent.

Nonetheless, it looked glorious to me. The leaves and flowers from that *Agave tequilana* individual became the first herbarium voucher that I ever pressed. It led me to initiate my own collection of plants, and to take a short course on field botany.

I had a rude awakening during that course; an older agronomy student playfully asked me, "What on earth motivated you to salvage this tattered wonder, and then offer it as a gift to us?" I had brought in several of my unnumbered vouchers to donate to the permanent herbarium of the University of Guadalajara, which has the largest botanical collection in all of western Mexico. I did not know which voucher he was referring to, so I moved closer to where he was preparing specimens for permanent mounting. He slowly opened two sheets of badly discolored newspaper to let me glimpse the desiccated agave lying there in repose. What had remained so gorgeous in my imagination had turned hideous, its flowers burned out like dead light bulbs.

Humiliated, I carried the specimen back home, hoping to resuscitate it. If I could only put the thousand shattered pieces of anther, pistil, tepal, and leaf together again like a jigsaw puzzle . . .

It was not long after that initial let-down that I returned to the University's herbarium as a student volunteer, intent on mastering botanical techniques. In the mornings I studied agronomy in the classroom as many young people did, but in the afternoons, I entered a world where the challenges were different: I wanted to solve the riddles of how to collect, press, and mount plant specimens without losing their essential character.

In 1982, while field collecting in the Bosque de la Primavera (Forest of Spring), I had another opportunity to collect and press an agave. I stumbled upon a plant not yet in flower; my attention shifted toward its bosom of leaves, each with chestnut-colored teats, tiny teeth, and an undulating terminal spine. As I removed a few leaves to press them, their serrated edges cut lightly into my arm, leaving their mark on me as they do on one another.

How lovely, I thought; this agave has a singular beauty, altogether different in texture and color from that of a cultivated blue agave. It was in fact another species, *Agave guadalajarana*, although I did not learn its true identity for several months more. My initial attempts to identify it were for naught, shackled by the contradictory, fragmentary, and altogether insufficient treatment of Jalisco's agaves in the older manuals we kept in the herbarium. These taxonomic treatises focused on few of the distinguishing traits that I could see manifested in the plants themselves. Fortunately, I was soon to have my problem solved. A friend handed me a compendium of information on agaves that had been recently edited by the University of Arizona Press. It was the lifework of an elderly plant explorer, Dr. Howard Scott Gentry.

Dreams Take to the Sunlit Trail

At first sight, what impressed me about the book was a picture on its back cover flap: Dr. Gentry sitting happily in the bosom of a giant pulque plant, *Agave atrovirens,* as if he had been born there, a vegetative offshoot himself. I tried to translate various passages of the book to quench my thirst for knowing which agave was which, but I did not yet have great faith that any book could help me overcome my underdeveloped botanical skills. To my surprise, I could use Dr. Gentry's keys with ease, and rapidly identified my second specimen as *A. guadalajarana.*

With the help of my professors, I established contact with Dr. Gentry. Soon afterward an invitation came to participate in the first-ever agave symposium to be held at the Desert Botanical Garden in Phoenix, Arizona, led by Dr. Gentry himself. He encouraged me to talk on the tequila industry, which I had already been studying when his letter arrived in 1985. About the same time I received his letter, I had the opportunity to help a remarkable team of researchers identify the agave species we had chosen to work with in Oaxaca. As I went back and forth to Oaxaca, Dr. Gentry's masterpiece on agaves traveled along in my suitcase next to a little bottle of mescal. On one trip, however, my luggage was temporarily lost. When I recovered my bags, they were drenched in the smell of mescal. The bottle had broken and the book had returned to me impregnated with the sweetness and smokiness characteristic of Oaxacan mescal. It was delicious to open, or to set it on my nightstand and close my eyes, taking in its aroma. Mornings of field collecting, afternoons of pressing and mounting, evenings of reading: the forms and colors of rosettes, succulent leaves, spines, teeth, and flowers danced through my dreams.

The Plant Doctor and His Apprentices

The day finally came for me to meet Dr. Gentry, my scholastic grandfather of sorts. With his blue eyes and Sonoran Spanish— echoes of my own clan—he was there at the airport waiting for me, ready to whisk me away to the Desert Botanical Garden for the agave symposium. Even his bolo tie reminded me of one my Sonoran-born father once wore. It was like a dream, for I was barely twenty-one and could not speak much English. I couldn't believe it, how this elderly man who had dedicated a large part of his life to agaves was now here to receive me, and to guide me.

When we arrived at the Garden, I realized that it was like an Eden for the diversity of agaves found around the Americas. This is what I had hoped for, a place where I could walk among them all, learning the various species one by one. Dr. Gentry walked along with me.

"¿Cual es su agave prefirido, doctor?" I asked him. He replied that *Agave ocahui* was his all-time favorite. We continued along, meeting agaves, meeting Dr. Gentry's students and disciples, and taking photos of him with each agave and each student who worked with one. I met Wendy Hodgson, Robert Bye, Susan Meyer, Suzanne Fish, and Gary Nabhan, who stepped in as my translator the next day when I gave my first lecture in the United States. Dr. Gentry playfully associated each of us with a particular species, not merely by what we studied but by perhaps more soulful connections as well. That was when he whimsically anointed me "Ana *Agave tequilana*," a species a little more common than the rest, and in my eyes, a little less attractive. Dr. Gentry was notorious for his gaiety whenever he encountered another person deeply interested in studying these succulent plants. "Welcome to the agave family!" he would write us.

During the entire symposium, Gary Nabhan sat by my side, quietly translating the gist of each lecture to me, wearing a bolo tie just as Dr. Gentry did. After the symposium, Susan Meyer served as my guardian angel, first taking me on a field trip to the red rock canyons of Sedona, then volunteering to do the technical translation of my talk to submit to a special agave issue of the magazine *Desert Plants*.

One Only Needs Patience

Late in his life, Dr. Gentry had valiantly tried to untangle the knots in the biosystematics of agaves, distilling his insights from many years of field collecting, and drawing on the patience he had gained through working among many cultures, under many conditions. These qualities allowed him to resolve some dilemmas in the evolution of agaves, especially as it has been influenced by humans, that most botanical researchers would not even dare to touch.

The road for the rest of us has been made easier by his work as a taxonomic *jimador;* we can now pass comfortably between the rows of thorny plants and see them for all that they are. We see the possibility of bringing Dr. Gentry's careful plantings to fruition. As the daughters and sons of Mayahuel, we have conspired together to complete the work that a moustached man in a straw hat and bolo tie began many years before we were born.

After a couple of drinks of mescal, Dr. Gentry once confided to us that Mayahuel spoke to him in his dreams, once encouraging him to build a network of botanical gardens at various elevations in order to conserve the genetic diversity of agaves. I believe that Mayahuel told other secrets to Dr. Gentry, secrets he took with him to the grave. Somehow, he was motivated, more than anyone who came before him or has come since, to weave his life from the earthly and divine strands of agave.

From 1935 to 1985, Dr. Gentry worked on many projects, from the cultivation of jojoba to the origins of the common bean, but his mind never strayed far from the riddle of agaves. He labored tirelessly, patiently placing each species in its appropriate section, iconizing it with its own ideogram, recording its history and its cultivation requirements, and compiling all records of vouchers from herbaria around the world.

A year or so ago, I returned to Arizona to take another look at Dr. Gentry's voucher specimens at the University of Arizona, which purchased them just before he died. As I opened up a folder and recognized his labels and his manner of elegantly laying out each agave on crisp, porcelain-colored paper, I felt my heart pounding.

There were Dr. Gentry's letters, written in his own hand—I began to hear his voice in them. There in the dried, perfectly arranged leaves and flowers, I could feel his conscientious and caring hand—it was all pressed into this voucher, one of more than a quarter million that he had prepared.

Then I opened a little note, which he had wrapped in a tiny paper package, tied with a silk string, and placed next to the label designed for him by his brother, a master printer with an eye for classical typefaces. Dr. Gentry had painstakingly recorded additional notes on the dimensions of each flower while it was still fresh, showing future workers that something is indeed lost when a plant is dried. And then as I sat scrutinizing these agave remains, Dr. Gentry's face, his white moustache and blue eyes, appeared before me. I realized that his handful of dreams was falling through the sunlight. I put my hands out, caught them, and held them amidst my own dreams.

Tochtecómatl: The Drunkenness Overtakes You

One evening when the daughters and sons of Mayahuel all ate together in the house of Howard and Marie Gentry, I could see how the old man studied all of us, watching to see if we needed any food or drink, curious about which of us were bonding. He was done with his lifework, and now looked after us like an attentive father, making sure he had a chance to speak with each of us, and to toast or to praise everyone in front of the others.

Just as agaves themselves are transformed into alcoholic beverages, Dr. Gentry succeeded in transforming us into a loosely working family, using a little tequila and mescal *bacanora* as lubricants. Mescal was the "nectar" that all of us drank, like migratory pollinators around an agave flower stalk. We laughed together like members of a far-flung family congregating for an episodic reunion; we all fell under the influence of agave, mildly drunk.

Dr. Gentry once commented that there were similarities between the coevolution of agave flowers with their pollinators, and agave beverages with their human consumers. He considered these ecological relationships to be symbioses and disliked the term "syndrome" to describe the predilection that nectar-feeding bats had for visiting certain shapes, fragrances, and flavors associated with particular kinds of agave flowers. Syndrome, he thought, sounded like a psychiatric term. "There is nothing psychopathic about it," he quipped, "this is nectar-feeding, not nectar-philia."

Both Dr. Gentry and I had also witnessed the ugly side of drunkenness, how it can damage relationships, and depress people so that they fail to express their finest qualities. The image of the *charro*, brandishing his bottle of tequila, and shouting his *grito* to the rainless sky, has dark, stormy elements to it at other times. But when I remember that first cloudless night that I drank mescal with Dr. Gentry, and we told one another stories of Mayahuel, I will remember the starlight, not the darkness. He took me out into the garden to show me the constellations, ones I could not see from the smoggy suburbia surrounding Guadalajara. He then confided in me something I will never forget. The message of Mayahuel, he told me, was that her dried-up bones are transformed into new offspring—all of her apprentices will eventually win the ancient game of Tochtecómatl.

It took me a while before I fully understood this message. Intellectually as a botanist, I knew that an agave "mother plant" literally dries up and dies while launching the only flower stalk she will produce over her life span, but that this dried stalk carries seeds and vegetative offshoots (bulbils) into another incarnation. And yet I did not understand this as viscerally as the old man did, nor did I know anything at that time about the ancient Aztec game known as Tochtecómatl.

Years later, I stumbled upon a discussion of this game by the eminent historian Miguel León-Portilla (1995), in his essay about Sahagún's compilation of codices taken from the indigenous communities around Lago Texcoco: "The profound spirituality of the Nahuas was based in their need to blend and to harmonize all aspects of their life, which they communicated in word and in deed, to reinforce their authentic feeling that [there] was indeed a unity in all of life. This impulse to unify into one pattern everything around them—manifested supremely in their cultural education, ethics, arts, law, calendar, cosmology, warfare and agriculture—also infused their diverse forms of recreation and play. Their games always manifested a symbolic character, [acted out by their players]."

León-Portilla then goes on to explain one particular game, which I suddenly realized was similar to the ritual that Dr. Gentry had attempted to emulate that night. In the game known as Tochtecómatl or "Bowl of Pulque," players were strictly prohibited from drinking any of the fermented beverage during the ritual. The pulque used in this rite was of the "fifth level," so called because five cups were enough to inebriate anyone. Those who participated in this game were the very ones who took care of the temples of the gods of pulque: the priest of the Two Rabbit god, who was the one who called all the players together; Patécatl, the priest dedicated to the cult of the god with the same name, who presided over the game itself; and the priests' apprentices, known as the representatives of the four hundred rabbits.

First, they placed in the center of the temple's plaza the "rabbit bowl" filled with pulque, and an icon of the god Patécatl. Then, they fit 203 hollow canes into the bowl, of which only one was secretly perforated.

The priests' apprentices representing the four hundred rabbits danced around the bowl throughout the night. When they abruptly terminated the dance upon hearing an agreed-upon signal, everyone in the congregation rushed in toward the bowl in search of the sole perforated cane. Whoever found it was proclaimed the winner of the game that night, and was able to drink all of the pulque in front of the rest of the group. Unlike our own ritual with Dr. Gentry, once the winner was completely drunk, the others retired before the sun came up.

To Keep the Faith Is Difficult, But It Can Be Kept

When I began to work with agaves, I didn't know how to get near them without getting stuck. Later, I could enter the densest, thorniest rosettes to measure their newly emerged leaves and I would not get hurt. Physiologist Park Nobel was the one who showed me how to get close to agaves, that is, live rosettes, not their pressed remains. We worked together in the field off and on for three years, following his invitation to help him study the effects of humidity, temperature, and soil moisture on the productivity of blue agave. The seasonal ritual of measuring agaves gradually brought me into a closer and closer relationship with the thousand-some individual plants that formed the study group for several experiments we maintained between 1985 and 1999. Park Nobel had a childlike smile and fascination with agaves, which gave me confidence that technical field studies of blue agave could be as fun as my first outdoor explorations.

"Faith," "patience," and "time" are words that I had never truly understood before. Sometimes when I am analyzing our data and something unforeseen appears, I feel like the agaves are laughing at me, reminding me of the mysteries that attracted me to them in the first place. They are testing how well I have come to play the game of patience. Suddenly, I am given permission to pass into their territory, to dwell there for a brief moment. They bow, and amidst their presence, I fulfill my work.

Acknowledgments

⁂

We first wish to acknowledge our indebtedness to the late Howard Scott Gentry for serving as mentor to both of us, and introducing us to one another over fifteen years ago. During that period of friendship, we have gathered with other "members of the agave family" many times, and our understanding of the plant/people interaction has deepened with this contact. In particular, we are indebted to Abisaí Garcia Mendoza, Robert Bye, Suzanne Fish, Wendy Hodgson, Park Nobel, Luis Hernández García, Edelmira Linares, Rodrigo Medellin, Ted Fleming, Liz Slausson, Luis Eguiarte, and Hector Arita for helping us feel part of a larger family of students of agave's interactions with people, bats, and pests.

We owe special thanks to María del Refugio Vázquez Velasco and Miguel de Santiago Ramírez for their excellent illustrations. Our other great debts are to our families, to our mutual friends, and to our editor and friend, Christine Szuter, for having patience and faith that this collective effort would bear fruit. Among those who traveled with us on this journey are Ana's sons Jorge Alberto and Jorge Luis, and her mother Guadalupe Zapata, Gary's daughter Laura Rose, and son Dustin Corvus, and a number of fieldworthy friends: Paul Mirocha, Laurie Smith Monti, Victoria Shoemaker, Liliana Madrigal-Plotkin, and the KUAT-TV crew. Botanist Dan Austin kindly assisted with nomenclature revisions.

We also wish to pay homage to the social scientists and historians who shared their knowledge with us, stretching this story in new and unforeseen directions: Rogelio Luna Zamora, José

María Murià, and Thomas Sheridan were particularly helpful. Rick Bayless, Jaime Morales, Patricia López, Rubén Ravelero, Patty West, Claudia Lopez Sanchez, Felipe Palma Cruz, and Richard Felger also assisted us with other professional perspectives.

Finally, the many fine professionals in the tequila and mescal industries offered us innumerable courtesies. Lic. Ramon Gonzalez Figueroa and his staff at the Consejo Regulador del Tequila, A.C., were unerringly supportive, as were many others at Tequila Tres Magueyes, Tequila Herradura, Tequileña, Tequila Cuervo, and Tequila Sauza. We also wish to express our thanks to the following for financial assistance for various binational conferences and projects in which we have participated: Agnese Haury, the Turner Foundation, the Turner Endangered Species Fund, Wallace Research Foundaton, Wallace Global Fund, Wallace Genetics Fund, W. Alton Jones Foundation, Pew Charitable Trust, C.S. Fund, Tequila Cuervo, and Hueblin, Inc.

We thank administrators and colleagues at the Universidad de Guadalajara, the Instituto Tecnologico Agropecuario de Jalisco, Northern Arizona University, and the University of Arizona for allowing us to devote time to this transborder collaboration. ¡Salud!

Tequila Hangovers and the Mescal Monoculture Blues

Gary Paul Nabhan

ᛝ ᛝ ᛝ

> During the several thousand years that man and agave have
> lived together, agave has been a renewable resource for food,
> drink, and artifact. . . . As civilization and religion increased,
> the nurturing agave became a symbol, until with its stimulat-
> ing juice man made it into a god. The religion and god have
> gone, but agave still stands as a donor species of the first water.
> —Howard Scott Gentry, "The Man-Agave Symbiosis"

I heard an aplomado falcon scream once above me. But mostly I
heard the sound of semitrailer trucks groaning through their
gears. Loaded with century plants, they were downshifting as they
ran the switchbacks into the barranca below. Near a train stop
called Cuervo in the Mexican state of Jalisco, I was ambling along
a volcanic ridge; the ridge was covered with row after row of the
century plants known as "blue agave." Their swordlike leaves had
been cropped back, but they retained enough spiny teeth to slow
the pace of my journey. The armored plants were both numerous and massive enough to cast a blue-green hue across the land
where I was hiking.

I trampled with marigolds, barnyard grass, and amaranths
coming up between the tightly cropped rosettes of blue agave but
could hardly penetrate the rows of the century plants themselves—and these were not just any century plants but the blue-
blooded king of all mescals, the highly bred species called *Agave
tequilana*. While the pruned tequilas sat only hiphigh, the un-

cropped ones at the lip of each terrace swung their swords up to my shoulders.

I looked up from the rows immediately before me and realized just how blue this world was. The next ridge over was also tinted with blue agave, as was the ridge beyond that. Far beyond was a minor outlying cordillera of the Sierra Madre Occidental. It too was blue with evergreen oaks and madrone seen at a distance. It was as if the local *mescaleros* had intentionally selected the blue agave out of the grayer or greener patches of agaves so that their plantations would match the color of the mountains on the farthest horizon. So they cut back the forest, replacing its many-hued cover with a powdery blue, opting for a color-coordinated world of their own making.

I turned around. Below me, a solitary mescalero was using a machete to thin the weeds overwhelming his agave patch. On the ridge above me, a dozen campesinos contracted by Tequila Sauza were armed with *coas de jima,* oval-shaped hoes with long handles. Each of these men would attack between 90 and 120 ripened agaves today, cutting back most of the leaves that had been produced over the past decade. They would manicure the thorny masses into blue-and-white pineapples, each *piña* weighing fifty to a hundred pounds. The men would then transform themselves into mules—their grim nickname for themselves—hauling piñas over to the semitrailer destined for the town of Tequila, where tons of agaves would be converted into gallons of alcohol. I was surrounded by blue-tinged ridges managed exclusively for the purposes of inebriating my fellow Americans.

I suppose I mean "my fellow Americans" in a way different from that with which LBJ began each of his speeches. I suppose I mean "all of my potential drinking buddies in the Americas at large." While a third of all tequila produced is shot down the throats of Mexicans, nine out of ten of the remaining swallows are destined for the bellies of gringos—U.S. and Canadian citizens. Tequila has been a global commodity since 1970, when its sales spread to more than forty countries. It has become more than that in the United States, the destination of much of the forty-seven million liters exported from Mexico; it borders on serving as some strange liquid currency between the psyches of the Mexicano and the gringo. As I was soon to learn, it has grown into what every American and Mexican business partnership dreams that its products will become. Certainly it is the dream of the North American Free Trade Agreement (NAFTA), poured into a salt-rimmed glass and chased with a lime.

A pickup truck rolled up to the Cuervo station, with Ana Guadalupe Valenzuela-Zapata barely visible above the wheel. What she lacks in height, Ana makes up for in other ways. She is a dark-haired, rosy-cheeked agronomist with unforgettable green eyes. We became fast friends when, on a whim, I volunteered to be her translator at the first U.S.–Mexico exchange of agave researchers hosted by our mutual mentor, Dr. Howard Gentry, about a dozen years ago. Since then, we have periodically rendezvoused to talk about the ups and downs of our personal and professional lives, always using the rise and fall of agave cultivation as the metaphor for what is happening in our respective worlds.

This time, as she drove me back from Cuervo station to the Sauza distilleries on the edge of Tequila, I asked Ana about the cross-cultural nuances embedded in the tequila trade. She laughed at my question and tried to shrug it off, but when she finally answered, her remarks sparkled with insight. "Remember that Don Javier Cenóbio Sauza—the one who consolidated the cottage industries of tequila making into a commercial agro-industry—was married to a woman from the United States," she said. "It was their collaboration that brought this provincial product into the United States in the 1870s. Now look at it: there are only about thirty companies legitimately distilling tequila in Mexico, but somehow their products are variously packaged into more than four hundred brands of tequila sold in the United States. Figure that out!"

When I first came to Tequila in 1977, the Sauza company was still using steam-heated rubble-brick ovens to roast the pineapple-like heads of agaves. Now, as Ana pointed out to me, Sauza exclusively uses autoclaves enclosed in thirty-foot-tall stainless steel vats. The other companies are converting to autoclaves as well, which are perhaps a more efficient way of cooking agaves to extract their sugars. But this technique requires considerable capital investment. Such capital flowed into Tequila only after the meteoric rise of the margarita cocktail, which has fueled the doubling of U.S. consumption of tequila since 1970.

"The tequila extracted from autoclaves . . . Ana, does it have the same taste as that coming from steam ovens?" I asked as I gawked at the giant vats of fermented mescal brew towering above me.

"It's hard to say, but we feel there's some loss of the smoky flavor. Maybe it's a taste that comes when a few of the piñas have been somewhat scorched in the steam-roasting. I've heard that autoclaved sugars never have the slightly bitter aftertaste found in the liquor expressed from roasted agaves fermented the old way . . . without a doubt, you can detect differences in taste between the traditionally processed mescal and the newer tequilas."

Until the late nineteenth century, the making of tequila was much like the making of other mescals. In fact, the distilled beverage made in Tequila's rustic backyard stills was not even called "tequila" until 1875. Before that, it was simply one of the many drinks known as *vino-mescal de tequila.* But Tequila's entrepreneurs helped this home-brewed hooch achieve the status of a specialty mescal, just as unblended scotch is no longer considered some mere run-of-the-mill whiskey—and the rest, they say as they tilt their glasses, is *"pura historia."* The vino-mescal of Tequila, Jalisco, became known world over as tequila proper, the hottest of all firewaters.

It was not until a century after tequila achieved this name recognition that Don Cenóbio Sauza and his competitor Don Jesús Flores began to modernize the distillation process, using technologies imported from the United States and Europe. Around that time, they also abandoned the underground conical pits that had been used since pre-Columbian times to roast mescal for food and for mildly fermented beverages. Those old conical pits were heated with many loads of oak gathered from neighboring woodlands. But once the extra-local demand for tequila began to grow, the distilleries sought out huge quantities of firewood, impoverishing the forest cover surrounding the pueblos of northern Jalisco.

The nineteenth-century deforestation of Tequila's valleys and ridges made the expansion of agave cultivation that much easier. The Sauza, Cuervo, and Orendain families encouraged thousands of campesinos to plant the blue agave instead of other mescals for food and fiber; many of these same farmers abandoned their milpas of maize and beans to work full time for the tequila industry.

It was then that an unprecedented tragedy struck their farmsteads. Social historian Rogelio Luna Zamora has chronicled how an epidemic devastated field after field. It was a plague that the mescaleros called the "gangrene of the blue agave." This was the first time that a plague of such proportions had appeared among agaves anywhere in Mexico. The culprit blamed for bringing a booming industry to its knees? The worm at the bottom of the bottle. It was a larva that burrowed into the heart of the plant, moving along (destroying agave tissues) until it had ravished its host.

This was just the first of many plagues to hit Jalisco, fed by the way in which the crop had expanded throughout the northern part of the region in less than a century. The larvae proliferated most rapidly where agave monoculture was most intense.

Perhaps the Mexican mescal plague was not as severe as the Irish potato famine, but it was an early warning against too rapid an expansion of a monocultural crop. This warning signal, says Ana, went unheeded: "José Antonio Gómez Cuervo, governor of Jalisco at the time, is said to have offered a prize of five hundred pesos of gold to the person who could discover an effective remedy for curing the agaves and liberating them from the plague. Yet the plague was stimulated by the very expansion and dominance of the blue agave cropping that his own family had promoted. At last, the plague subsided a bit as campesinos learned to trim back infected leaves and destroy the larvae in them."

Ana sighed, as if dizzy with the larval feeding frenzy that had gone on in her imagination. "I'm afraid the agricultural industry somehow forgot the message of that plague. Sadly, it is happening all over again, but this time, the mescaleros say that the agave plants have AIDS, not merely gangrene."

As far as scientists like Ana can tell, the blue agave plantations have been suffering from an outbreak of multiple maladies since 1988. At least two bacteria and one fungus are running rampant in the agave plantations, causing stems to rot and leaves to dry up and wither. The plantation workers call these problems *marchilez, secazón,* and *el anillo rojo* because the latter turns the leaves from slate blue to yellow with rust-toned bands encircling them. As the plants begin to wither and die, a puslike goo oozes from the leaf tips. But the plantings are also infested with weeds that harbor insects—the very insects that carry diseases from one agave to the next. The weeds also compete with the agaves for sunlight and water, further adding to their stress and, ultimately, to their susceptibility.

Before Ana and I had left the fields near Cuervo station, we had rolled over one after another of the recently cut piñas; they were rotten to the core. Many of the untrimmed plants still standing showed the telltale signs of larvae boring through their leaves. Most of the piñas cut from the fields through which I'd hiked would soon be rejected at the distillery, for they had too little uninfected tissue to cook and ferment. The fields casting their delicate blue over the volcanic landscape of northern Jalisco were degenerating into a muddy brown, spoiling from the inside out.

Ana's hunch is that this multiple-malady plague has been driven by rapid overexpansion in the planting of just one vulnerable variety, the blue agave. In less than a decade, the land covered by this single, vegetatively propagated clone of tequila expanded from 40,000 acres to nearly 120,000 acres. About the time these plantings began to reach maturity, prices dropped precipitously, for overproduction had led to a buyer's market. Plantation owners could no longer afford to invest more money in tending their plantings. Their fields became infested with weeds or even abandoned altogether. Soon, the plague had driven tequila prices to a new high.

The bacterial diseases first caught hold around 1988 in the higher elevations. They did not appear in significant numbers in the lower terraces and valleys until 1994. Now, the "SIDA del agave tequilero"—the AIDS epidemic of the blue-blooded century plants—is reported at every elevation, in well-managed fields as well as in abandoned ones.

The way blue agave plantations have been managed undoubtedly served as the environmental trigger to this plague, but there is also a genetic vulnerability in this narrowly selected variety of agaves. Today, vegetatively propagated clones of blue agave make up more than 99 percent of the 150 million agaves growing in Jalisco. If there ever was an easy target for any infestation, tequila monoculture is it.

As late as 1977, varieties of four species of century plant were regularly mixed and roasted together to make the mescal that the rest of the world called tequila. The blue agave variety was already dominant but not ubiquitous. When an elderly mescalero named Juan Gonzalez Encisco took me through the fields and holding areas of mescal harvests destined for the Cuervo distilleries, he pointed out many representative plants of the other varieties, ones that are rarely found in commercial operations today.

Old Juan waxed eloquent about these other heirloom mescal varieties: *sigüín,* the only race still with an indigenous name, known for its small, roundish form and early ripening; *chato,* or *saguayo,* a large squat mescal with a thick flower stalk and fibrous leaves; *bermejo,* a tall mescal with many leaves; *moraleño,* a shiny-leafed plant with showy qualities; and *criollo,* a wild-looking plant similar to those growing in the barrancas. Ana has learned of other varieties as well, some of which have resistance to the insects and diseases attacking the blue agave, among them *mano larga,* "the large hand"; *zopilote,* "the vulture"; *pata de mula,* "mule foot"; *azul listado,* "blue listed"; and *mescal chino,* "Chinese mescal."

Today, outside the gardens that Ana herself has planted for conservation purposes, it is difficult to find a full row of any one of these other varieties. Official norms of the Mexican government regulating the tequila industry have put pressure on growers to plant blue agave and nothing else, even though the presence of these other varieties slowed the spread of diseases in the past. After each tightening of government regulations—first in 1972, then in 1978, and finally in 1993—the factory purchasers of ripened agaves became more and more reluctant to let the other varieties slip into the heap. The ten or so other heirloom varieties native to the Tequila vicinity no longer account for even one in a thousand plants there; when they are kept at all, they are usually grown for hedge, fiber, or ornament.

Ana, who is accustomed to swimming upstream against the current—first as a female agronomist in male-dominated terrain, then as a conservationist in a domain framed by short-term profits—is fighting to change the reliance on only one genetic strain of agave. Her dream is of another Jalisco, one not so blue.

It would hold in place a more diverse range of agaves than she sees around her now.

And so Ana went back to school, hoping to gain a few skills that will help change minds, not merely farming practices. She has pursued a second master's degree, this one in business administration, to help her with a most peculiar kind of business. Her thesis is devoted to the planning of a museum and botanical garden aimed at conserving agave diversity and preserving traditional knowledge about mescal cultivation and use. She envisions a botanical garden full of all the folk varieties of agaves remaining in Jaliscan plantations, hedgerows, and house yards, as well as all the wild species of the Sierra Madre. She has collaborated with her sister, a young architect, on blueprints for a museum that will someday chronicle the cultural significance of agave diversity from pre-Hispanic times to the present, replete with archives of historic documents, exhibits, and demonstrations of traditional processing techniques. And the two sisters imagine a "museum without walls" with meeting rooms and an auditorium where mescaleros can come and tell their own stories.

In the meantime, she has not forsaken her science. All one summer, she was busy measuring and recording the diagnostic characters of the remaining folk varieties from plantlets she propagated more than a decade ago. These dozen surviving folk varieties of cultivated agaves are not the only family members in danger. Another forty-eight wild species in the agave family are imperiled in Mexico; several more are threatened in the United States and Guatemala. In most of these cases, the destinies of the century plants are linked to those of indigenous cultures whose foraging and horticultural practices have nurtured them for centuries. Few agave species grow in habitats completely untouched by humankind; most have been the subject of cultural as well as natural selection. They have, over the centuries, adapted to the burning, tending, and terracing of the indigenous drinkers, weavers, and landscapers who have shaped the Mesoamerican terrain.

Will Ana's efforts make a difference in the tequila industry? It is more likely that some of the biggest tequila makers will instead invest in planting thousands of clones, tissue-cultured in laboratories where they have been genetically engineered for resistance to the prevailing pest or diseases of the moment. The cloning of tequila plants, unfortunately, will never raise the eyebrows that the cloning of sheep has raised. On the other hand, such cloning will never give the tequila industry as much security as would heterogeneous fields where several species of agave grow in close proximity to one another. Ana's vision of agave genetic diversity depends on buyers at the distilleries caring whether the farmers with whom they work are buffered from wildly varying yields and prices.

♠ ♠ ♠ ♠ ♠

Not long before this visit with Ana in Tequila, I had the horrific experience of being stranded in Los Angeles traffic for hours against my will. At the time, I was so weary that I couldn't figure out how to escape this metropolis in which I knew no place to rest.

It was much like a story from Kafka: as my car inched forward, I doubted that I would ever get free of all the asphalt, concrete-reinforced bridges, barricades, overhead lights, and glowing metal signs. I saw no vegetation, no animals, no handmade objects. There were few signs that "life" actually existed, other than the thousands of cars moving through the twilight. I could see humans only through their windshields darkly.

We all seemed to be going down the same chute as rapidly as we could, but I could not for the life of me fathom where we were going. All the exit names seemed vaguely familiar; they were the names of towns or suburbs found all across America: Glendale, Ontario, Riverside, Inglewood, Lakewood, Garden Grove, and South Gate. I could have been anywhere in the United States. The sameness made me sick to my stomach, sick and enraged in my head, sick and sad at heart.

That same sense of sickness came over me as I looked at all those rotting heads of blue agave, pineapples spoiled by their own monotony. Yet I did not think of the plants themselves as sickening; I felt that they were a symptom of some larger disease of contemporary societies, especially those that promote or even accept only sameness.

Fortunately, that nightmare had a counterpoint in my imagination—a dream that Howard Scott Gentry had passed on to

Ana and me. Dr. Gentry, who spent forty years of his life collecting and studying agaves, acted as mentor to Ana and me at a time when we felt like nothing but strays. We both needed to come under some elder's wing. Dr. Gentry not only encouraged us in our field studies but also offered us inspiration through the stories he would tell. Many of those stories emerged over shots of mescal during our late-afternoon get-togethers in his garden.

For all the adaptability he had developed while traveling as a plant explorer, Dr. Gentry never learned to sleep in the city. A dream or nightmare would often wake him in the middle of the night, and he would remain awake, pondering its significance for hours. Fortunately for us, he wrote one of those dreams down. In it, he had been told by his U.S. government employer that his agricultural duty station had been transferred. Instead of basing his work as a plant explorer out of USDA headquarters, he was to move to Mexico to establish a genetic conservatory for all the agaves in the world. It would be located at Tepoztlán, an awesome montane landscape south of Mexico City. There he was charged with designing a means to keep all the various forms of mescal alive in one place.

When he arrived in Tepoztlán, he could not believe his eyes. The Mexicans had fashioned a huge elevator to move agave plants up and down the cliff face above the village. This elevator moved not only vertically but horizontally as well. It allowed Gentry and his colleagues the mobility to place each agave species in the micro environment to which it was best suited. By matching up agave species from all over Mexico with niches on the cliff face or within the barranca below it, Gentry's team was able to tend the full gamut of century plant diversity, from tropical jungles to coniferous forests, all in one locality.

Gentry never saw his vision bear fruit. "It was," he would say, taking one last swig of bootleg mescal, "just a dream."

But I'm sure that he wanted it to happen. Ana's plans would have made him deeply happy. Who knows whether the tequila industry will ever share such a dream, but I am sure there will be others who will help Ana keep it alive.

Before we left Tequila, Ana drove me around the town in search of a statue I had once seen. This statue—of Mayahuel, the goddess of agaves—was an icon that had enchanted Dr. Gentry,

Ana, and me one afternoon as we leafed through a book of Aztec codices. The last time I had seen the statue, someone had stolen the copper-blue agave out of Mayahuel's hand; she had looked forlorn, nearly desperate, left without her very reason for being. A goddess with no flame to keep. Now, with another plant placed within her grasp, Mayahuel seemed once again full of purpose. I hope that when I visit her again one day, I will find her in the midst of a place no longer painted with monotonous blue but resplendent with a full palette of colors.

Note

Tequila, once called *mezcal de tequila* in Jalisco, is one of many kinds of *mescal,* a term sometimes spelled with an *s* in the U.S. borderlands but always with a *z* in central Mexico. In this book, we use an *s* throughout for the term in its various forms except for brand-name products that use a *z.*

¡Tequila!

Distilling the Essences, Blending Two Worlds

⁂

The Heart of the Family

The agave family can be found scattered over a large stretch of the Americas, growing from southern Canada clear to the Andean highlands (García-Mendoza 1998; Gentry 1982). What most Anglo-Americans recognize as "century plants"—and what most Mexican-Americans call *"maguey"* or "mescal"—are the sword-leaved succulents in the botanical group or genus *Agave*. Mexico is the heartland for this family of succulents; it is where the agave arose as a divine character, a caloric gift, a magical cure, and as an inebriated curse upon a dry and stony ground (Gonçalves de Lima 1978). Although most of this story is set in Mexico, its actors range beyond the Tecuexe Indians and Tapatio countrymen of Jalisco to include Filipino sailors, bootleggers, Yanqui railroad moguls, plant explorers, songwriters, European industrialists, botanical taxonomists, and the lords of English pubs and breweries. Just like the diversity we find in the botanical family known as the Agavaceae, we have found that diverse cultures and characters have been attracted to these plants, enriching their history.

The Agavaceae is a botanical grouping with less than fifty years of recognition as a coherent assemblage of kindred plants (Gentry 1982). Agavelike plants have been placed in one family after another as various botanical classification systems have risen and fallen. And yet, the genus *Agave*, first recognized by Swedish botanist Carl Linnaeus, has persisted in much the same dimensions over the last two centuries. Agaves characteristically form short-stemmed rosettes of succulent, sharp-pointed leaves, and persist several years before flowering and dying. The rosettes can be solitary, but oftentimes agaves have an older "mother" rosette with smaller "pups" or vegetative offshoots extending from her skirts via underground rhizomes. Each rosette is monocarpic, that is, it flowers once, withers, and dies.

While the taxonomic identity of the genus *Agave* is easy to resolve, the shifting taxonomy of its close kin makes it seem as though they are going through an identity crisis. Other, similar-looking plants in related genera have been moved back and forth from the Liliaceae to the Amaryllidaceae, to the Agavaceae in the broad sense, as it was recognized in the 1960s and 1970s (García-Mendoza and Galván-Villanueva 1995). More and more sophisticated genetic, biosystematic, and cladistical analyses have begun to elucidate the origins and affinities of agaves, yuccas, and their kin (Álvarez de Zayas 1995; Eguiarte et al. 1997). Under the scrutiny of these new tools, the size of the Agave family has shrunken, as a number of species have "departed" to join the recently recognized Nolinaceae. Families break up and re-form among plants as they have among humans.

Nonetheless, most of us who have seen a mature agave in flower will never confuse it again with a yucca, or worse, a cactus or aloe. Although all of these botanical wonders may be water-conserving succulents, each has its own characteristic flowers, as well as its own history, geography, and spirit.

Deep in the heart of this history, geography, and spirit lie Mexico the republic, Mega-Mexico the floristic region, and Meso-america the cultural region. Here is where 80 percent of all species of *Agave* in the world find themselves most at home (Gentry 1982). Here is where the many threads of the natural and cultural history of agaves are most tightly woven together, forming a tapestry that portrays the legacy of humans in the shape of the agave on one side, and the imprint of agave leaves on the destiny of cultures on the other. To gain a sense of how intricately agaves were woven into human culture, one only needs to consider the extensive vocabulary developed in the Americas simply to speak about human interactions with these plants (see appendix 1).

Long before the Columbian Exchange shattered former patterns of human and botanical geography on a global scale, wild and domesticated agaves had already joined the ranks of the most widely and intensively used plants in the Americas (Gonçalves de Lima 1978, 1990). The number of agaves domesticated by prehistoric cultivators in the Americas is truly impressive (see appendix 3).

Ironically, the Columbian Exchange did not usher in the demise of agaves as it did for other Native American crops such as amaranths and chia. Agaves were transformed by new technologies into one of the most important rural economies surviving through historic times into contemporary Mexican society. And now, tequila and other mescals inspire barroom singing around the world, not just in the land of the charros. Tequila has flowed out of the rich, volcanic Mexican earth into the markets (and mouths) of many peoples, all around the world.

Agave-Culture

When a new term is coined, it is best to define it in a way that will make its usefulness last for centuries. So let the term "agave-culture" do what no other word, phrase, or description has done: let it root itself in the land, and flourish for many years to come. Agave-culture is a cluster of plant husbandry techniques, harvesting practices, and ritual observances specifically intended to foster the growth of plants in the genus *Agave*. It brings together traditional ecological knowledge about these plants, and the diverse ways they may benefit humankind. Traditional knowledge embedded in agave-culture has for centuries kept alive dynamic interactions between biodiversity and cultural diversity, manifesting themselves in the myriad uses of heirloom varieties or *razas criollas*.

The range of cultural uses of agaves is staggering. No wonder the Nahuatl term *"metl"* that was used for agaves implied that they were the miracle plants of Mesoamerica—*el arbol de las maravillas*. Motolinia, one of the earliest European observers of agave-culture, testified in the *History of the Indians of New Spain*, that the uses of agaves were endless (García-Mendoza 1998; Gentry 1975, 1982). He offered an inventory of these uses as if it were a litany: *aguamiel* (the fresh nectar beverage), pulque (the fermented nectar), syrup, vinegars, string, cordage, rope, shoes textiles, nails, paper, thatch, tiles, fuel, soap, bandages, and snakebite cures.

These many uses have spawned an enormous literature celebrating the cultural legacy of agaves. The number of codices, ethnobotanical treatises, and technical reports devoted to agave-culture could completely fill a good-sized museum.

Consider the following agave initiative by the Mexican government's Secretary of Promotion, Colonization, Industry and Commerce in 1884:

> With the goal of promoting the study of the different kinds of agaves that are produced in our Republic, and to form a basis for a compendium about these little-known but fascinating plants, so that we can showcase a collection of these plants at the next World's Fair in New Orleans, we are asking each municipality in the entire country to provide us with three medium-sized plants of each wild and cultivated agave in their reach. (Luna-Zamora 1991)

Since time immemorial, the indigenous cultivators of agaves have developed and refined a body of traditional management knowledge that has adapted different agaves for the production of pulque, fiber, or mescal. Some of these horticultural wizards have sophisticated strategies for genetically selecting distinct varieties of agaves for their suitability to the elaboration of particular products: fiber, food, nectar, or distilled beverages. Looking at a list of pulque agave varieties from the turn of the nineteenth century, you can see how each selection had its unique value, from its morphological characteristics, to the quality of its nectar and time to maturity.

Another important aspect of agave-culture is how each variety was custom-fit to a particular set of agronomic practices adapted to peculiar landscapes. At least that is the case for the agave production practice known as "*sigh-saa-leiz*" in the Zapotec Mayan tongue. "Sigh-saa-leiz" can be translated as "agave-stone-string bean" (García-Mendoza 1998). It describes an ecological dynamic between the giant pulque-producing maguey *(Agave salmiana)* and string beans, when they are intercropped on rocky slopes. This is but one of many examples we will explore in depth in the following chapters that demonstrate how sophisticated particular traditional practices are in selecting agaves to fit specific ecological conditions (Valenzuela-Zapata 1985).

Maguey or Mescal?

The beverages produced from various agave species can be divided into two broad groups, based on how they are prepared. Those that are derived from liquid sugars draining out of a scooped-out flower stalk are known as "aguamiel" when left unfermented and as "pulque" when used to produce alcohol through yeast fermentation. Those that are elaborated by roasting the entire "heads"—leaf bases around a central caudex—are collectively known as "mescal" once they are distilled. When the roasted heads are mashed and left to soak in yeast-laden water, they produce fermented but undistilled beverages variously known as *mescal crudo, tesquino,* or *tiswin.* The latter two names are of Mediterranean, perhaps Arabic origin, brought to the Iberian Peninsula by the Moors, and to the Americas by the Spaniards. Tequila is simply one kind of distilled mescal made famous in one Mexican landscape, just as scotch is a kind of whiskey made famous in Scotland.

The ancient terms *"maguey"* and *"henequén,"* once specific folk names for particular species of agaves, were heard for the first time by Europeans upon their arrival in the Antilles (Álvarez de Zayas 1995). Later, these terms were applied generically to edible and fiber-bearing agaves, respectively, and accompanied conquistadors and colonists on their journeys across the American continents. The cultural diffusion of these Pan-American terms for agaves could serve as the sole subject of a book-length text on agricultural history. These portmanteau terms carried by colonists have partially replaced the many indigenous terms for agaves, some of them elements in sophisticated folk taxonomies constructed by native gatherers and farmers with discerning eyes for genetic variation.

For example, in pre-Columbian times the many Mayan-speaking groups in Mexico, Guatemala, and Belize developed a binomial classification system (much like the Linnaean system) that distinguishes one fiber-bearing agave from another (Colunga García-Marín and May-Pat 1997). *Sac ki* signifies white henequén (*Agave fourcroydes*), in contrast to *yax ki,* which is green henequén (*A. sisalana*). Other parallel examples abound; for instance, the Rarámuri (Western Tarahumara) nomenclaturally distinguish truly wild *A. angustifolia* from a culturally selected tequila-like variant grown in hedgerows that botanists place in the same species (Bye, Burgess, and Tryan 1975).

Somewhere between three and five centuries ago, the term "maguey" began being used throughout Mexican territory as a generic or distributive term for all agaves. At the same time, the term "mescal" persisted in the north as a general term for all agaves with "heads" suitable for roasting. The term "amole" became used in the north for all nonedible, sapogenous (soap-bearing) spicate agaves, which are typically used as medicines as well. Curiously, the majority of producers of the blue tequila agave in Jalisco use "mescal" for describing their own plants, and reserve the use of "maguey" for describing the giant pulque-producing agaves grown nearby.

While many histories speak of the discovery of pulque-making from aguamiel and the distillation of mescal as one and the same, these two processes have dramatically different origins and destinies. The plants selected for each process are quite different as well. Pulque agaves are of extraordinary dimensions, with enormous leaves large enough to cradle a grown man (Gentry 1982). They are thick, juicy succulents of the altiplano "highlands," selected as cultivated varieties within several different species (Parsons and Parsons 1990).

The indigenous inhabitants of Mesoamerica and Aridoamerica (to the north) have been chewing the sweet sugars out of agave fiber quids for more than nine thousand years, as confirmed by the "coprolites" (fossil feces) found in caves (Gentry 1982). This pit-baked form of nutrition—once called *mexcalli* in Nahuatl—can still be found in regional markets throughout Mexico, where it is now sold simply as mescal, the roasted leaf bases and heart (caudex) of agave. As the Aztec term "mexcalli" evolved into the Hispanicized *"mezcal"* then "mescal," it came to be applied not only to the roasted food-stuff, but also to the distilled beverage derived from it, and to the crop that engendered it. The mescaleros who transplanted and tended particular varieties for pit-roasting selected them for shorter stalks; thicker leaf bases; softer, longer fibers; more rapid maturation; and higher palatability after roasting. They also selected out those clones with toxic compounds and high sapogenin content, intentionally planting more of the vegetatively propagated stock from mother plants that proved to be sweet, stout, and full of stamina. At least a dozen wild species were domesticated through clonal selection to meet the needs of mescal-making (see appendix 3).

Of course, in some regions of Mexico, the inhabitants refused to grow agaves only for pulque, only for mescal, or only for fiber. Oaxaca and Chiapas form one such region, where rich cultural and biological diversity are packed into the semiarid sierras in a manner that sustains all three agave industries, nearly side by side.

The prevailing notion has been that the process of distillation was completely unknown to ancient Mexicans, but this has been challenged by a few archaeologists and ethnobotanists who point to rustic stills made entirely of pre-Columbian technologies, surviving in the hinterlands until today (Bye 1993). Nevertheless, even these scholars would concede that distillation was neither widespread nor the most common means of preparing alcoholic beverages prior to the Conquest. Curiously, it appears that three sailors, not European missionaries, may have been the first to introduce distillation to the agave-growing inhabitants of Mexico's west coast (Bye, Burgess, and Tryan 1975; Bruman 1935). Before that fusion of Old World technologies with New World wonder plants, most mescaleros produced alcoholic beverages simply by yeast-fermentation of agave sugars, without the additional steps involved in distilling off the essences. The Filipinos brought sugar cane to the coast of Jalisco and Oaxaca, and along with it, brought the distillation of rum or *aguardiente* (Bruman 1935; Walton 1977). The backyard technology for making cane sugar into firewater became the model for transforming pit-roasted and fermented mescal into the first *vinos de mescal,* as they were originally called.

The concept of mexcalli, the native wellspring of nourishment, was then transmogrified into the mescal of the mestizos, the potent fuel for inebriation. There is no doubt among historians that the seeds of the distilled mescal phenomenon first germinated in two distinctively different cultural landscapes, one where indigenous influences continue to flavor it (Oaxaca), and one where the prevailing flavor comes from *mestizaje,* the blending of foreign and indigenous traditions (Jalisco).

The differences between these two traditions are palpable as one travels northward from Oaxaca through central Mexico, to Jalisco. It is not a rare occurrence to be able to find small-scale mescal-makers vending their wares in the open air markets or *palenques* of Oaxaca. In Jalisco, the scale and sophistication of distillation found near the town of Tequila today would be unrecognizable to José Cuervo, who lived there a century and a half ago. Machine-packaged cases of tequila are stamped with international standards of quality (ISO 9000) after the liquor itself is passed through a biochemically precise process in stainless steel vats the size of water towers.

Nevertheless, these are not the only two mescal-making traditions that will survive into the twenty-first century. From the clandestine bootlegging of bacanora in Sonora (Bahre and Bradbury 1980; Borewell 1995; Sheridan 1988; Nabhan 1985) to the hacienda-style local production of *mescal de la olla* in the highlands of San Luis Potosí and Hidalgo (Parsons and Parsons 1990), the cultivation and distillation of regionally adapted agaves still fill an economic niche in many rural economies.

Mescal and Tequila

Under Mexican law, there exists a legal distinction between mescal and tequila, although both "spirits" have gained some protection under "Denomination of Origin" legislation. In more general terms, however, there is a difference in the kinds of agave utilized and the region where the production of each is based. The first mescal to be codified and recognized by its own geographic origin was that of tequila. The regions of origin for other mescals vary, and extend across much of Mexico: Durango, Guerrero, Oaxaca, San Luis Potosí, and Zacatecas. Today, however, other distinctive mescals have become recognized by their particular names and flavors: San Carlitos from Tamaulipas; bacanora from Sonora; *tuxcacuesco* from Jalisco; and *raicilla,* also from Jalisco. Bacanora has recently received a go-ahead for establishing its own Denomination of Origin, and raicilla makers are also in the process of securing their own.

At another level, the pragmatic difference between tequila and all other mescals is a matter of scale. Even in the region of Oaxaca where the most mescal de la olla is produced, its total export value in 1994 was only US$445,990, compared with the $156 million sale of tequila the same year (INEGI 1997). This difference in scale has allowed the tequila industry to market its products through a variety of strategies that add value to its distillate: handcrafted bottles, brightly colored labels, and special tags all heighten its mystique. The market niche for tequila is no longer the border town cowboy; it is the sophisticated businessman who seeks organic, naturally grown products, handcrafted folk objects, as well as exotic flavors and fragrances with aphrodisiac qualities!

The choice between drinking a cured tequila and a bootleg mescal is purely subjective if not subliminal. For that matter, what attracts anyone to drink mescal instead of whisky or brandy? Flavor? History? Mystique? Devotees sense that mescal is the stuff from which legends are made. The romance-laden, rustic labels found on most brands of tequila today attempt to reinforce this sensibility. What other contemporary distillate attempts to echo ancient indigenous myths from the days when the Americas were still wild, still filled with mystery? Drinkers are lured to tequila not so much by its proof as by its promise—a promise to reconnect them with something earthy, primal, and native. A shot of tequila, like a good story, beckons us to come join others in a journey where unforeseen adventures lie ahead.

Mescal de Tequila

The Mexican-American Microcosmos

ł ł ł

The agave is the most precious gift Nature has given to Mexico. ... Tequila gives its name to the distilled spirits of mescal, just as cognac has given it to the liqueurs of France.
—Dr. Ernest Vigneaux, *Souvenirs d'un Prisonnier de Guerre au Mexique*

Wearing the Right Paternity Suit

To assign the story of tequila to the back pages of the history of pulque is to write a false biography. Until recently, such histories have confused different members of the same agave family, and blurred cultural regions where different agaves have traditionally been grown. Somehow, they have even confused beverages derived from completely different organs of agave plants. In short, casual histories written by journalists-turned-instant-agavologists have too often obscured one easy-to-observe fact: the roasted blue agave of the Jaliscan highlands and its distilled essences have formed a cultural legacy altogether different from that of the giant Mesoamerican magueyes, their upwelling juices called aguamiel, and their yeast-fermented beverage, pulque.

Mestizaje Means Cross-Pollination

Unlike pulque, which can claim a prehistoric Mesoamerican origin, tequila's evolution is not purely autochthonous. Like *mole poblano*, tequila is a mix of indigenous and Hispanic elements that slowly fermented during the protohistoric period, only to rise to its fully leavened state well after the Conquest. Like the offspring of Cortés and Malinche, of Mayahuel and Dionysius, tequila is *puro mestizo,* a hybrid with a vigor all its own.

However complex its origin may be, tequila has become one of the fuels driving the vehicle of Mexican identity. Tequila is a blended fuel, mixing the energy extracted from the blue agave by the native *jimador,* with that of cane sugar expressed from the introduced *trapiche* pressing mills. Once industrial distillation was introduced to Jalisco, promoters suddenly elevated the mescaleros of Tequila from the lowly ranks of menial laborers whose only wares were staple foods and fermented beverages, to the status of alchemists, who magically capture high-proof spirits in a bottle.

The elaboration of tequila has been dramatically shaped by a creole techno-culture. At first, it was merely a cottage industry practiced by mestizos who labored in fields and distilleries in the service of wealthy *hacendados.* However, those gentlemen-farmers soon nurtured international business and social contacts that helped them usher in further technological innovations and marketing strategies.

Los Charros: A Made-for-TV (and Tequila) Identity

Within this new techno-culture, a new prototype of Mexicanicity incubated and hatched. As social historian Alfonso Alfaro (1994) suggests, the earliest phase of this hatchling looked very much like "el charro" in classic Mexican "cowboy" movies: "These rural aristocrats—cattlemen, maize producers or tequila plantation owners—were all horsemen at heart. They found in the Charro lifestyle the most natural and distinctive expressions of man; they found in the white heat of tequila the quintessential taste of the land, one which flavored their entire aesthetic. They dwelt in a universe defined by a love for the aroma of the very earth itself, by the shadows fixed in a brilliance emanating from an unyielding sun, and by words said once, and once only. Theirs was sensibility and an exuberance emphatically masculine."

Mayahuel, Goddess of Curing and Blurring

Perhaps that is why these charros raised above them, in a prominent plaza situated near the heart of Tequila, an unflinchingly romantic statue of the goddess of agaves, Mayahuel. According to Gonçalves de Lima (1978, 1990), this goddess was among the most important deities in the Aztec pantheon, for she was associated with inebriation, dance, and curing. It is claimed that Mayahuel was once truly human, but was made immortal and transformed into the embodiment of agave's sacredness. From the moment she was made divine, her juices encouraged lactation among women of all ages, and she became a mother to them all.

As Mayahuel is represented in the *Fejérváry-Mayer Codex*, she is seated at the heart of a large agave, nursing a child in her arms, the flowers and fruit of the plant emerging from her torso. Sometimes, as in the *Vatican A-21 Codex*, her face is bicolored indigo and gold, her skirts also indigo, and she holds a cup brimming with flowers. Judging from the frequency with which she can be seen in the few surviving codices, Mayahuel can surely be counted among the most popular deities in all of Mesoamerica.

Nevertheless, it must be remembered that Mayahuel was already an old lady when the first charro got hungover by drinking too much mescal. She is much more tightly associated with the ancient traditions of pulque and aguamiel than with the post-Columbian eruption of tequila and other mescals. As products elaborated through technological processes that did not even take hold until well after the Conquest, tequila and its kindred mescals have become imbedded in a set of art forms entirely different from those of the classic Mesoamerican codices. They are the liquid currencies that charge the charro films with their masculine energy, and which run through popular poster art plastered on cantina walls and calendars, paperback romance novels and *fotonovelas*. Tequila and mescal can be heard bubbling up into ranchero and mariachi music. These images first shaped the regional identity of those who lived in Nueva Galicia—Jalisco and its surrounding highlands—and then cast Mexico's national identity into an altogether unprecedented form.

Did Tequila's Domestication Take Off Only After the Conquest?

As for the plant itself, the blue tequila agave was also shaped into

something somewhat different from all other domesticated agaves in Mexico. Its intensively cultivated varieties were clonally
selected to produce the best results in the context of extensive
rain-fed (nonirrigated) agriculture, and in the industrialized distillation plants of the emerging techno-culture. Despite the fact
that tequila is not purely indigenous in origin, history, technology or image, this hybrid product has become something mar-
velously consistent with the new Mexican identity. Tequila and
its popular techno-culture are microcosms of the new Mexican,
of national pride. At the same time, they have reinforced Mexican machismo, keeping alive a place in the collective imagination
where a man can claim to be the owner of his world, where he is
at once gallant and gentlemanly, and an incurable womanizer.
Thus, the feminine deity Mayahuel has largely been replaced in
tequila techno-culture by saleable icons of romantic masculinity.

Tequila's history is not purely natural; it is also social. It can
be examined through various lenses—psychological, sociological,
political, ecological, or economic. Despite all the scrutiny tequila
has already received from Marxists, feminists, and structuralists,
no one has completely circumscribed its place in Mexican identity.

What Does the Word "Tequila" Want to Say to Us?

According to historian José María Muriá (1990), there are many
interpretations of the original significance of the place-name
"tequila," with interpretations ranging from "place of labor" to
"obsidian quarry site." The interpretations that he feels have the
most etymological veracity is "the place where cutting is done"
and "the site where certain kinds of labor are accomplished." The
place-name is no doubt etymologically related to the Nahuatl
terms *téquitl,* meaning "work, position, employment, fatigue," and
tlan, meaning "place of." The term *tequio* is used in rural Jalisco
today to refer to labor on behalf of another, just as the Nahuatl
term *tikpan* does. Perhaps the first meaning is closely associated
with the farmwork of cutting the leaves off agave plants, or to the
jima or harvesting of ripened plants. For well over a century, the
landscape of Tequila has been characterized by the agrarian activities situated there, for the labors of the jimadores are more
frequently seen here in the area of tequila's origin than anywhere

else. Agaves require an unusually specialized sort of labor; both the knowledge and tools of the jimadores are unlike those applied to any other crops in the region.

The second meaning proposed by Murià may also refer to means of managing this perennial crop. The "certain kinds of labor" are the processes forming the profound ecological relationship between the region's human inhabitants and this succulent crop. This interrelationship is what Howard Scott Gentry (1975, 1982) called the "man-agave symbiosis," for it set up an interdependency that has changed the trajectory of both human society and this domesticated succulent in the Jaliscan highlands. There, the name "Tequila" is given to the town, the municipality, the surrounding valley, and the most prominent mountain overlooking the landscape (Murià 1990). Today, the smokey fragrances of tequila-making pervade the entire blue-tinged valley. The "wine of mescal" elaborated there, is now known by no other name than that of its place of origin, just as its local consumers in cantinas became known as *tequileros* during the last century.

Why Does Tequila Loom Large in Our Imaginations?

The poets, historians, folklorists, and singers of the Americas have held up a bottle of tequila as a way to look at the world in front of them, and they have found tequila to be a prism, a mirror, a chimerical presence. For ethologist and essayist Luis Barjau (1997), tequila "is a drink as fresh and as genuine as the clean Sunday clothes of native folk on the way to church. And yet, the illusion of tequila as something inherently evil, has become a theatric device, expressing malevolence as swiftly as the image of a lip so dry that a piece of cheap cigarette paper sticks to it; as a wayward curl of black hair falling out from the edge of a sombrero; as a glimpse at the cross-eyed gaze of beady black eyes like those of a field mouse, or a pair of papaya seeds inextricably stuck together."

There is a Mexican proverb, or *dicho*, that states, "Para todo mal, mescal, para todo bien, también" (For all things bad, take mescal, and for all things good as well). Tequila and other mescals have been prescribed to cure loneliness and melancholy, but as Malcolm Lowry's *Under the Volcano* (1971) eerily demonstrated, it can plunge its devotees into even deeper isolation and gloom:

"The real cause of alcoholism is the complete baffling sterility of existence as *sold* to you."

Mescal on the Move

Regardless of whether *mescal de Tequila* was worthless as a cure for loneliness and melancholy, its drinking rapidly spread beyond Tequila's cantinas, Jalisco's state boundaries, and Mexico's sovereign territory. By the 1870s, it had transcended being a purely Mexican drink, and had made its way in bottles and barrels to the United States and Europe. Except for the special but limited cases of its brothers, bacanora and raicilla, tequila is the only mescal to have left its generic name, "mescal," behind, and to be greeted internationally by its first name, "tequila." For a brief period in the late nineteenth century, both Sonora's bacanora and Jalisco's various vino-mescal variants were all marketed to U.S. citizens on equal grounds. Tucson, Arizona's Julius Goldbaum sold them all—even locally produced agave moonshine—as "Mexican brandy," "Mexican whiskey," "mescal wine," "liquor of mescal," and "mescal de Tequila." Then Cenobio Sauza's mescal won the "Columbian Exposition Brandy Awards" at the 1893 Chicago World's Fair, and the drink became famous enough to depend on the name "tequila" alone, both within and beyond Mexico.

Tequila and Romance

The tequila industry has been in full flower for well over one hundred years, and its distilled spirits are never found alone—they are always reflecting other images around them, like a ball of mirrors over a barroom floor. Images from films, songs, and novels veer into the scene. Tequila never gets to offer its soliloquy, and it seldom makes a solo, cameo appearance. Mariachis in charro suits are always intruding, reinforcing some latent stereotype of the Mexicano. To search for the forgotten one, to console the jaded lover, one need only to head for the cantina in a Mexican film from the forties, and tequila would already be there to guide you. As Jose Alfredo Jiménez cries out in one such cantina, "Those who have never arrived in a cantina needing a tequila or a mescal, well, . . . they are telling me to forget myself, for now I hardly know if I have any faith left, but now I can only pray to them to knock another time to see if she has gone."

Like an anaesthetic, a permanent euphoria, or a continuous fiesta, tequila stays with you. As another Mexican proverb reminds us: "Borrachita de tequila llevo siempre el alma mía." (A little drunkenness of tequila always fills my soul.)

The linkage between tequila, romantic music, and handsome singing charro cowboys—among other Mexican myths—probably emerged as a fitting medium for holding the collective aspirations of rural Mexicans. Social commentator Enrique Serna (1995) has shown us how this myth, emerging in the thirties but blooming fully in the Mexican films of the forties, has incorporated a wide variety of regional mythic elements within it. As Serna says most succinctly, "the Jaliscan essence has been fully expressed by these tenuous desires." Like the gaucho of the pampa and the buckaroo of the Wild West, the icon of the charro has spread around the world, taking his tequila along with him.

The Mexican microcosm has traveled outward in bottles, barrels, video cassettes, CDs, and film canisters to all parts of the world; the charro legend is part of our planetary folklore, dispersed through the process of the cross-cultural borrowing that now surrounds us all.

The Wild Origins and Domestication of Mescal de Tequila

‹ ‹ ‹

In the past, various Mesoamerican cultures considered agaves to be sacred plants, to the degree that they were thought of as divine beings, such as the goddess Mayahuel. Their juices, their flesh, their fiber, and their life were so important to the survival and cultural development of various human communities that they could not have existed without agaves and their relatives.
—Robert Bye, "The Role of Humans in the Diversification of Plants in Mexico"

An Island of Persistence for an Ancient Tradition

Twelve hundred kilometers north of Tequila, Jalisco, on an island in the Sea of Cortés, there is a circular, stone-lined pit for roasting mescal that is perched high on a ridge above the crashing waves and salty drifting mist. Dense patches of agaves, cacti, and ironwood trees proliferate around the pit today, for it has not been used much over this last century compared to previous ones. Prehistoric pottery shards as thin as eggshells, stone knives, and the charred bones of land iguanas and sea turtles litter the ridge top where a clearing once existed. Past the pottery, past the knives and the bones, we are following an elderly man, who is walking, sometimes stumbling. He is moving back in time, returning to the ancient origins of mescal.

The old man, whose name is José-Juan Moreno, is slowly ambling over volcanic cobbles, an agave stalk for a cane in one hand, a newly captured iguana in the other. He lives on the coast of Sonora some forty kilometers away, but he has come to the island many times over the last six decades, accompanied by his Seri Indian relatives, by archaeologists, and by botanists. He is among the last of his hunting and gathering tribe who is expert at selecting and roasting mescal, and this is his favorite place to harvest ripened wild agaves.

However remote this place may seem from Tequila's cultivated fields and mechanized distilleries, we are witnessing here an ancient tradition that underlies the entire industry of mescal production. José-Juan Moreno is in his seventies, but his way of gathering agaves has been practiced in this region for more than seventy centuries. As he stops to look beneath an ashen-colored rosette of spine-tipped leaves, he is revealing to us the very roots of agave-culture.

The plant that captures Moreno's attention is a clone belonging to the subspecies known as *Agave cerrulata* ssp. *dentiens;* it is known only from Isla San Esteban and Angel de la Guarda in the Sea of Cortés (Gentry 1982; Felger and Moser 1985). Moreno refers to the plant as *"heme"* when conversing in Cmique Iitom, the Seri Indian language now spoken by less than five hundred of his kin. But his ancestors who lived on Isla San Esteban also had an affectionate nickname for this plant: *xica istj caitic,* "soft-leaved thing" (Felger and Moser 1985). They would rely upon it as an emergency source of potable fluids during extended periods of severe drought, and unlike other agaves, its heads could be cooked year-round and were easy to pull up from the ground. Its leaves would be cut off, roasted over coals, and scraped and then pounded in a sea turtle carapace until liquid was extracted. It was said that the resulting beverage was sweet and satisfying, not unlike pineapple juice.

Moreno crouches, catching his breath, and examines a large rosette that sits like a head of cabbage on a short stalk rising up among the cobbles. Then he shakes his head disapprovingly, and continues his ramble, rejecting one plant after another. We are amidst thousands of wild, freely cloning agaves, but he is searching for the select few that are fully ripe.

He seems unfazed by the blistering heat. Although the autumnal equinox has recently passed, high noon on this island feels like a Midsummer Day's nightmare—one that some perverse Shakespeare might dream up for a play set in the Islas

Encantadas. Magnificent frigate birds are circling above us, and sea lions grunt and snort on the rocky shore below us. None of this, however, distracts Moreno from his task. Finally, we guess, he has found the plant of his desires. He motions us to come over to where he kneels next to a large plant.

"See this terminal bud, how thick it is, how broad its leaves are?"

We nod, assuming that this is the character to search for in ripened plants.

"It's no good! It's not yet ready to harvest! But look here, next to it—this one is. Its leaves are getting thinner, more pointed. This plant will soon flower. Now let's take it with us!"

One of us dislodges two large cobbles of lava from beneath the giant head, while another pries it up with an axe and a couple of poles. With the axe, we sever its rhizomal connection to the rest of the clone, uprooting it and rolling it toward the old man.

"Now, trim away all the leaves except for this one!" We cut through the succulent leaf bases with our knives, and soon the cabbagelike rosette has turned into a pineapple. When we are done, Moreno leans over, and makes an incision halfway down the sole remaining leaf. He then slices the leaf upward from this horizontal cut, until his knife reaches the terminal spine. He strips off the waxy epidermis on the backside of this leaf, takes the two straplike products of his labors, and ties them into a knot. Suddenly the sole remaining leaf has been transformed into a durable loop of fiber, a simple handle by which the agave can be carried overland.

Once two agave heads have been shaped in this manner, each is looped over opposite ends of an agave stalk, which is used like a yoke to carry the plants back down to the beach. One of us suffers the consequences of *not* using such a yoke: shouldering a trimmed agave without any protection, enough juices drip down to cause a burning sensation and skin rash. Since we are carrying the agaves more than five hundred meters back across volcanic cobbles, around cacti, and down steep slopes, an agave stalk yoke allows the journey to be completed with minimal effort and pain.

When we return to Moreno's home village, dozens of his neighbors are there to meet us on the shore. "Here come the mountain travelers!" they chant, as they have done for centuries when anyone returns from the rugged mountain islands (Felger and Moser 1985). The iguana that Moreno captured for dinner causes as much commotion as the agaves themselves. Young, long-haired men help us carry the pineapplelike heads over to a roasting pit that they had dug the day before.

Once ironwood branches and bark chips have been burning for several hours, Moreno orders the men to toss the agaves atop the red-hot coals. Slowly, rocks are placed atop the upside-down pineapples, and then dirt is shoveled in around them to cap off the pit. The temperature of the roasting pit is checked throughout the afternoon and evening, and again the next morning. By midday, the pit is partially opened so that the color of the smoke and the extent of charring on the agave's exteriors can be evaluated. Moreno determines that the baking has been thorough and that the agaves are ready for dismembering into small pieces the size of a tamale. That evening, after a short speech, Moreno offers the rich, caramelized baked agaves to his fellow villagers. They savor every sweet, smoky morsel that passes through their lips.

The Geography of Wild Mescal Harvesting

From the northern rim of the Grand Canyon of Arizona to the lowland tropical forests of Guatemala, agaves have been pit-roasted for food over the last eight to ten millennia (Castetter, Bell, and Grove 1938; Fish et al. 1985). What the Seri Indians still practice today is part of an old hunter-gatherer tradition that once extended from Baja California, clear across the Mexican mainland to Tamaulipas. Different species were harvested, each with their own seasonality, but the prevailing pattern was the same: mature agaves were selected, trimmed, placed atop a bed of coals, covered, and baked for one to three days. The resulting product, *mescal tatemado,* could be eaten immediately, stored for later use, or fermented into a beverage poor in alcohol content but rich in flavor. Rituals evolved to accompany the unearthing of the baked agave hearts, or the passing of the communal cup of fermented mescal. Mescal, in whatever form it was consumed, always offered more than mere calories and soluble fiber for ingestion. It offered a taste of the primal elements, for earth, fire, and water imbued every mouthful (Heyden 1983).

The wild-harvesting of agaves by hunter-gatherer folk like Moreno gradually evolved into the cultivation of selected clones, and the elaboration of distilled beverages. Even in the Seri Indian tradition called *quimozxa*—the pilgrimage made to harvest mescal—the initial stages of horticultural management of agaves are evident. Entire plants are not uprooted and destructively harvested; instead, a few mature "branches" of a clone are selectively pruned, while the clone itself lives on. Moreno scrutinized every rosette of a certain size class, selected just a few, and then severed their rhizomal connection to the "mother plant." He, like most farmers, are curious about morphological variation within plant populations. And his pruning techniques for agaves are not unlike what an orchard-keeper might apply to his fruit trees. Agaves may branch differently than fruit-bearing trees, but they still branch; pruning away one rosette as it reaches maturity is fundamentally no different than managing the growth trajectory of a grapevine or an apricot tree.

Envisioning the Early Domestication of Agaves

Moreno and his Seri kinfolk still refrain from actually farming agaves, even though other cultures—from the Anasazi of the Colorado Plateau and Aztec of the Valley of Mexico to the Hohokam of the Gila River and the Paquimé of Chihuahua's Casas Grandes—readily embraced their cultivation. At some moment in the remote past, a woman or man took one of the rosettes, trimmed off an agave clone, and replanted it in a place where it could receive better care. Or perhaps a vagrant agave took root on its own, after being uprooted, carried to camp, then neglected at the edge of a dumpheap. While the rest of the same harvest was roasted and eaten, this one survivor rerooted, and grew into a plant robust enough to merit the attention of some innovator, who emulated the process by planting other agaves in the fertile ground surrounding the dumpheap (Gentry 1975; Hernandez-Xolocotzi 1993).

It may well be that the motivation for increasing the local abundance of agaves had something to do with their perceived scarcity (Bye, Burgess, and Tryan 1975). Perhaps as the local human population grew, the wild agaves had been too frequently pruned relative to their growth rates—this Malthusian dilemma could have triggered investment in cultivation. Alternatively, perhaps some prehistoric family moved from a place where agaves were abundant to one where other resources were available, but not agaves. Out of a fondness for mescal, they returned to their former home, unearthed a few rosettes, and carried them to a place where only cultivation was an option.

Such speculations are seldom satisfying to those intrigued with archaeological puzzles regarding the origins of agriculture, unless they have been sipping mescal. Then, sooner or later, it seems as though the pieces of the puzzle fall together, and the picture of the past comes into perfect focus. We can hardly take a time machine back to witness the incipient domestication of agaves, unless that vehicle is fueled by mescal.

Once prehistoric cultivators regularly began to tend transplanted agaves, other possibilities emerged (Bye 1993). They found that any interesting clonal variant could be easily separated and propagated to produce other plants with the same desirable characteristics. Undoubtedly, those agaves that cloned more prodigiously and matured more rapidly were automatically favored by cultivation. Other traits were more consciously selected. Farmers favored plants with smaller terminal spines and fewer lateral teeth on their leaves, as well as those that lacked caustic juices. Because most food agaves were also used for their fiber, farmers sought out clones with more pliant leaves and stronger, longer fiber cells (Parsons and Parsons 1990).

Although plants derived from the same clone may at first glance appear identical to one another, peculiar characteristics always arise among a small percentage of clonal offshoots in both the wild and in cultivated fields. These "sports"—what geneticists now term "somaclonal variants"—can be readily detected by someone tending a patch of agaves, and if the variant is a desirable one, it can be easily propagated and "fixed" in the population (Garibay 1988; Sánchez-Armenta 1991). Gardeners around the world have observed somaclonal variants—a red-and-white striped onion amidst a batch of pearly white ones, or a cluster of round tubers amidst a field of oblong potatoes. Agaves are no different from other crops that can reproduce from seed as well as from vegetative (nonsexual) propagation. They have a remarkable capacity to express new variation, and once farmers find something that strikes their fancy, they can rapidly increase the favored variant through vegetative means.

Nevertheless, the process of agave domestication is not well documented in the archaeological record of Mesoamerica and Aridoamerica, for the morphological changes from wild to domesticated stages were not as dramatic for agaves as they were for maize, beans, or squash (Fish et al 1985; Bye 1993; Nabhan 1994). A teosinte or wild maize plant moves from one generation to the next during a single rainy season; the life cycle of an agave spins more slowly, and the changes wrought within a single human life span are barely discernible. Nonetheless, over a dozen agave species have evolved under the domestication pressures exerted by indigenous farmers, and they now appear to be distinct in many ways from their wild progenitors.

Unraveling the Taxonomic Knot

Ironically, the wild ancestry of the blue tequila agave has been obscured until recently, for taxonomic ambiguities and a poor archaeobotanical record from western Mexico have made hypothesis testing difficult for those scientists interested in such issues (Rivera 1983; Valenzuela-Zapata 1985, 1997). Local folklore in the *zona tequilera* simply asserts that the blue tequila agaves were originally recruited from nearby barrancas, a plausible but untested hypothesis. In fact, several wild species of agaves persist in the barrancas of northern Jalisco and adjacent Nayarit, and others nearby may just as easily have been involved in the domestication process. In addition, there are vague descriptions of agaves that could either be wild or cultivated, such as some of those that botanist Trelease encountered between 1907 and 1920 in Jalisco, included in his treatise *Los Agaves de México* (Gentry 1982).

While Gentry concluded that many of the taxa described by Trelease did not merit recognition at the level of species, they may nevertheless provide clues to the domestication process. It appears that prior to the late nineteenth century, several land races or *razas criollas* were cultivated in the Tequila region for use in mescal production. It was only late in that century that the blue agave cultivar emerged, having been intensively selected for its short maturation cycle, and baking qualities that were compatible with more industrialized processing. At the same time, some of the land races and family heirloom selections described by Trelease, Perez, and Blanco began to disappear from field-scale cultivation; perhaps the semidomesticated links between wild types and fully domesticated cultigens disappeared during the last century as well (Perez 1887; Valenzuela-Zapata 1997; Franco-Martinez 1995).

While most botanists could agree that the blue tequila agave was one of several economically important species among the Rigidae section of the genus *Agave*, most of them conceded that its progenitor could be any one of several rigid-leaved species with paniculate inflorescences. It was not until Gentry's (1972, 1982) comparative analyses of floral traits in the genus that one could discern that blue tequila agaves fell well within the morphological variation of the widest-ranging paniculate agave in the Americas. Nevertheless, nomenclatural problems obscured this fact. In the 1970s, Gentry (1972) still referred to the widest-ranging wild species on the west coast of Mexico as *Agave pacifica*, and did not recognize it as the same species as the domesticate called *"espadín"* by the *magueyeros* who produce mescal in Oaxaca (Rivera 1983).

Then, in his 1982 masterwork, Gentry recognized that this single, wide-ranging species, which he called *Agave angustifolia* Haw., was composed of both wild and cultivated varieties. When we assisted him with his geographic gazetteer of herbarium collections known from Mexico and Central America, it became obvious that this one highly adaptable species ranges from one hundred kilometers south of the Arizona-Sonora border, all the way to Guatemala, Belize, Salvador, Nicaragua, and Costa Rica, from sea level to fifteen hundred meters in elevation. It is one of the few species that ranges from the Atlantic coast of Tamaulipas all the way to the Pacific coast of Sonora, and from the northernmost to the southernmost states in the Republic of Mexico. Gentry's (1982) concept of *A. angustifolia* was ever-changing, and did not reach equilibrium before his death, some fifty years after he first observed these plants.

A year after Gentry's magnum opus was published, while reviewing the nomenclatural history of *Agave angustifolia* Haw.,

Dutch botanist D. O. Wijnands (1983) suggested that the earliest valid name published for this agave was assumed to be given to it by Carl Linnaeus, *A. vivipara* L. Nevertheless, American botanists do not recognize the historic precedence of the name offered by Linnaeus, as Australian botanist P. L. Forster (1992) did when he described several horticultural cultivars as varieties of *A. vivipara* in the journal *Brittonia* a decade later. That is because *A. vivipara* is only valid as the name having precedence for what has otherwise been called *A. cantala,* a domesticate distinct from other narrow-leaved agaves in the *A. angustifolia* complex.

It is now clear to us that not only is *Agave angustifolia* Haw. the earliest valid name for the entire complex of narrow-leaved, yellow-to-green flowering agaves, but that many cultivated varieties are derived from this wild gene pool as well. Since many of these varieties (including the blue agave clone) have the capacity to produce viviparous bulbils on their inflorescences, this name is not only nomenclaturally valid, it is also memorable in a descriptive sense.

Gentry (1982) admitted that *Agave tequilana* botanically belonged within this complex species, but was hesitant to formally synonymize the name for this cultigen with that for the wild species. He wrote that "*Agave tequilana* is distinguished from its close relatives in *A. angustifolia* by its larger leaves, thicker stems, and heavier, more diffuse panicles of relatively large flowers with tepals long in proportion to the relatively short tube. . . . Since these differences are of degree rather than of distinct contrast, their separation as a species is nominal, but appears tenable for the Rigidae, where species are so hard to define. Certainly, the commercial trade with this important economic plant will profit from the maintenance of this simple binomial."

Ironically, as we shall see in future chapters, commerce has *not* profited in recent years by treating the blue agave clone as a separate entity from the larger, more diverse gene pool that once formed the basis of mescal production in Jalisco, as it has in other states. While the species in this group are hard to define, it is evident that far too much "splitting" has occurred historically, obscuring evolutionary relationships and peculiarities that have resulted only under domestication pressure. Gentry was, however, clear that there was little taxonomic difference between the blue agave of Jalisco, and similar domesticated agaves found in other states, including Oaxaca.

We have striven to complete the work that our mentor Dr. Gentry began in recognizing the relationships between these wild and domesticated forms of the same taxon. In appendix 4, we propose a comprehensive taxonomic revision to recognize one highly variable subspecies within this narrow-leaved agave complex, and one polyphyletic subspecies of cultivated varieties whose distinctive traits (larger leaves, thick stems, and robust flowers) are ones easily influenced by cultivation.

One particular feature strikes us about this description of the historic spectrum of mescal varieties found in Jalisco and elsewhere. As we will reflect upon at other times in this volume, many of these varieties are known from just a handful of flowering specimens, and some are now exceedingly rare as field-scale plantings (Franco-Martínez 1995). There has been an inexorable tendency to invest in the spread of the blue agave clone at the expense of other time-tried elements of genetic diversity. With the recent spread of diseases among the plantings of this one clone, an epidemic that we will discuss further in later chapters, tequila producers are finally reaping what they have sown, thereby threatening the cornerstone of their entire industry.

Tillers and Tale-Tellers

The Agrarian Tradition of Jimadores

ᛐ ᛐ ᛐ

"El mescal es muy delicado," he says. "Muy celoso, muy limpio,"
talking as if the liquor is a person who had to be placated and
pleased."
—Thomas Sheridan, *Where the Dove Calls*

Tuning in at the Cantina

While listening to the keepers of tequila's agrarian tradition, one
must sort through a legacy laced with as many myths as facts.
Mescaleros are forever spinning yarns about mescal—the plant
and the spirit—while working in fields or resting in the nearby
shade, and while jiving on the street corner or drinking in the
cantina on the village plaza. They keep up their running commentary while bolting for cover during a sudden downpour, or
cursing the sun as it bakes the plants they have tended for seasons.

When those who can speak to tequila's trajectory and destiny unleash their passion, time does not pass, but past, present,
and future occur simultaneously. To speak in the tongue of a
mescalero is to let a river flow without detaining it, no dam, no
immediate destination.

A mescalero commences his commentary in a husky voice,
barely above a whisper, offering at first only the tersest of phrases
and explanations. Slowly, and laboriously, he begins to weave together impressions and experiences into an elegant tapestry. As
his story wanders, his audience's appetite is whetted by his precise expressions and by their own drinking-in of mescal and
words. They begin to trail along, moving through the field with

him, listening to his observations about each plant, while hearing the sound "trap" as the agaves themselves speak back. As they pass more and more plants, moving down the rows faster and faster, they hear the snapping open of the leaf buds, "trap!/trap!/trap!/trap!" That is, they catch the very sound of the agaves themselves unfolding with a flush of new leaves emerging with the blessed rains. And then, the men no longer concentrate on the voice of the mescalero himself, for they hear only the agave plants speaking to one another, rejoicing as the harvest nears.

The Quixotic Nature of Oral Tradition

There are some storytellers who are graced with a fine memory for details, recounting that which has been passed down from generation to generation of tequila-growers; they retain valuable information that has yet to appear in any agronomy text or written history regarding tequila, the plant, and its cultivation. Nonetheless, it is more common to hear stories that are told simply for the benefit the tale-teller and his social and economic allies, stories that uphold their particular biases about the tequila business. Fortunately or not, there are usually others present who will argue the opposite merely to discredit the more self-serving of storytellers. Even if one were not able to decipher all the nuances in a barroom debate about tequila, it would be possible to discern which mescalero is actually honored by his peers. By the end of the night, the one who truly knows the most about mescal has been offered the most complimentary drinks by his compadres. In the thick of the yarns, however, it is typically hard to tell who is wholly fabricating their own history, who is guarding certain secrets, and who is diverting attention away from their own ignorance as means to achieve their own ends.

Diminishing Interest in Doing It the Old Way

It is the elderly men who undoubtedly know the most about cultivating the blue tequila plants, even though much younger men now dominate the work in the fields. These elderly mescaleros are seldom seen helping with the cultivation today, but they have paid their dues, toiling long years in the fields. They can be found almost any night speaking to their sons about their experiences—

admitting their failures, reflecting upon their innovations—as a means to guide the younger generation.

At present, however, they speak to an audience with diminished interest in their wisdom. It is clear that attending to the traditional arts of mescal cultivation and distillation have waned as the industrialization of tequila has intensified. The funds of traditional knowledge about mescal cultivation is being replenished only among the most independent of small-scale farmers, and even they must occasionally take on additional work as day laborers for the larger operations. Today's tequila industry is less and less likely to recognize their diligent attention to tradition, or to purchase their modest output of high quality product. While we personally have always sought the counsel of the elderly men who grew up working the fields of Tequila or Los Altos, these men are listened to less and less today. Even their own sons barely give them respect; nor do they give credence to the notion that a farmer's way of life will ever again be worth much socially or economically.

The older craftsmen in the art of tequila cultivation feel their influence waning. They look at their sons and sadly admit that "if their only goal is to pack a wallet full of dollars, it might be better for them to get their backs wet [crossing the border] than to bake them in the sun here at home."

The Dry Season

There is no escaping the fact that the art of producing quality mescal will always require a considerable investment of manual labor. This is especially true in the months just prior to planting, as well as the months in the midst of the rainy season. The need for both manual labor and mechanized tillage intensifies as the year proceeds from April's dryness to October's drenching of greenery.

At the onset, the workers must prepare the vegetative offshoots for planting, separating them from the mother plant, maintaining them in a temporary nursery, then transporting them to their destination within the plantation. Then, as the season proceeds, additional tasks are added to the schedule. April, the cruelest month, arrives. Its heat and dryness tans, burns, and blisters the skin of mescaleros. There is barely a cloud in the sky to buffer the fieldworkers from the sun's intensity. Their feet sink into the talc-like soil, broken open and baking. What soil the men don't work by hand is churned and turned by tractors pulling plowshares, harrows, and rakes.

If April's winds prove unrelenting, the parched soil is easily whipped up into dust devils that pelt the skin of anyone who remains unshielded from their assault in the field. Over time, the assailants' faces become pocked and creased into deep furrows. Even when sombreros are worn to shelter them from the onslaught, their ever-reddening necks cannot escape the weather-beating. Whenever mescaleros pause in their labors during the heat of the dry season, they wipe away the salt stinging their eyes, and try to refocus. But as they reopen their eyes, they see that a heat mirage still wavers on the horizon, and the ache in their heads still drones like a thousand cicadas at noon. There are some who suffer unmercifully from such solar exposure, breaking out with heat rashes so wretched that they cannot return in short order to the labor that wins them bread, wine, and soothing remedies.

When "hunger weather" rages down on tequila fields like this, the mescaleros can escape its rigors only by shifting their hours, arriving in the twilight before dawn. By six in the morning, all of them are fully embroiled in the tasks at hand. The work crews, called *cuadrillas* (squadrons), are expected to keep working right through the peak heat of the day. Nevertheless, by nine in the morning, one or two workers get restless and wander out of the fields to gather a few dry twigs for a cook fire. They heat up a sheet metal *comal,* place it over a meager bed of coals, and prepare a makeshift "brunch" at the field's edge. There, the entire squadron comes together to eat, as well as to rest, and as they do so, they rekindle their debates from the day before. Their debates, of course, concern themselves, more often than not, with tequila, women, religion, or politics, or in some weird way, all of the above.

It is during such lollygagging that the bulk of extant folklore about traditional agave culture is transmitted, down to its finest details. It is done as the men are sitting amidst their tools and their dogs, hungrily waiting for the food to be warmed. The men have already emptied their plastic bags of the tacos and tortillas that they have brought from their homes; they have sautéed their chiles and beans, and once everything looks ready to eat, they hunker down to savor their meal. As the daily fare is consumed, a few of the men offer black-humored commentaries to the others, who have crowded beneath the little shade they can find. This shade, this refuge, this sanctuary of oral history often comes in the form of a *parota* or parrot tree. It is magnificent tree that forms a giant canopy, a mythical tree known elsewhere in Latin America as *guanacastle* and known by botanists as *Enterolobium cyclocarpum*. It is the only woody plant for miles in any direction that offers a modicum of shade. The parota is a patch of relief from the unremitting sun in an entire landscape of sun-drenched blues. During the months of April and May, the dry pods of the parota are toasted over the coals along with the tacos and tamales, preparing their seeds for eating with salsa and salt.

The Day Wears On

After their brunch, the fieldwork recommences. The campesinos say, "farmwork framed by short bouts of rest always yields the best." When the sun burns down on the work crew, they must make time for breaks, and to ensure that everyone has drunk enough water, the crew boss passes around bottle-gourd canteens plugged with corncobs. The gourds keep the water tasting fresh and cool even late into the day.

While some workers carry on a lively banter among themselves all day long, there are those who refrain from speech altogether, believing that "you dry out your mouth and lose all your breath." On harder days, it is only when the sun becomes no more than a blot on the horizon, and the men's clothes are drenched with sweat and stained with salt, do they quit, before their "heads begin to boil."

The workers take to the road as soon as they have gathered up their tools, lunch sacks, and canteens. They walk back to the place where they had congregated in the morning, bid one another farewell, and depart for home. They have swapped enough words to know the plan for the next day, and by late evening, they have their tools cleaned and sharpened once again for the upcoming tasks.

The Rainy Season

During the more humid months of May through October, the brutality of the searing sun diminishes. The earth becomes fragrant and the fieldwork less exhausting. A dew covers the herbs of the field each morning, drenching the work shoes of every man. Mists relieve the weariness the mescaleros have been shouldering day in and day out for weeks. Episodic thunderstorms hit with such force that they finally must abandon their work for a spell.

About that same time, the cobblestone roads around Tequila get undercut by floods and fall into ruins. The old jalopies used by field crews constantly get stuck in potholes that begin to look more like muddy wells. The mescaleros carry towing chains, jacks, and come-alongs to pull their trucks out of the perilous ruts. Within each crew, there are always one or two men who become expert at rescues, and at navigating through such pitfalls and potholes on their way to the tequila fields. The red clay gumbo soils stick like glue to the tires. Mud coats every cobble. Trucks bump and grind over every stone until the stones themselves disappear. Suddenly the driver finds himself out of control, sliding down into the fields where only the largest agaves can break their fall.

It grows increasingly difficult to complete even the most routine fieldwork as the rainy season drags on. The unrepentant rains and impassable roads disrupt any task that the men attempt. Keeping the weeds down is the first and foremost duty, but even this becomes impossible, so they turn to herbicides to reduce their labors in *el cazangueo* and in the *limpia de coa* (see appendix 1). Migrant workers carry backpack sprayers so that they can apply a variety of herbicides to inhibit growth of the weeds, while others use tractors to disk the weeds under.

While soil moisture is still high, they also apply fertilizers. But at the same time, when the heat and humidity are high, conditions are ideal for insects, which eat the young leaves, and for larvae, which come out of the soil to eat and infest the roots of agaves. To combat this, the men apply insecticides—some of the same chemicals used to treat rootworms and earworms on corn.

When tequila is booming, you can find lots of people in the countryside, putting in new plantations. Pickup trucks carry the planting crews out from the villages even before the first light of dawn. Storms still come through every few hours, but a radiant sun warms the workers in between the tempests. Plant growth accelerates. The landscape changes from an ashy color to an intense blue-green. The rank herbs come on like a headache for the land owners, who insist that their mescal plants not be "shaded out" by weeds.

And then, the rhythm of work wanes as October comes on. Over three-quarters of the year's rainstorms have already come and gone, leaving roughly 60 centimeters of moisture for the soils to suck up. At last, it becomes easier to move through the gaps between rows, which are no longer pooled with mud and wild with weeds. The moisture is held deeply in the volcanic soils, and the surface dries out, permitting the men to finish the weeding and pruning tasks that have eluded them for weeks. The campesinos work hard to rid the field of the last flush of weeds, which have begun to dry up, for if they are left they run the risk of carrying wildfires through the plantation. It is well into November before all the fieldwork feels like it is under control.

Agrarian Traditions of Managing Agaves

With the exception that ceremonies in thanksgiving for a good crop are seldom practiced today, the cultivation of blue agave is maintained through traditional techniques passed down from one generation to the next through a code of oral instruction and demonstration. The cultivators constantly refer back to traditional funds of empirical knowledge when discussing details in the selection and preparation of soils for planting, or in the selection of vegetative offshoots for replanting. They have also worked out optimal densities of agaves for field plantings, which are remarkably close (within 2 percent) to what physiological ecologists have determined to be the theoretically optimal densities for multiannual biomass accumulation in agaves (Nobel and Quero 1986; Nobel 1994).

The practical guidelines for managing the soils, crop growth, pests, and weeds in agave plantations have all been derived from traditional practices, and all continue to have validity. Even the tools used—with the exception of tractors, discs, and backpack herbicide sprayers—are ones that have been designed in the zona tequilera, and are forged only by local blacksmiths.

The selection of particular cultivated varieties for planting by mescaleros was largely accomplished within two different historic eras when domestication pressures on the plants were most intense. The first era was when indigenous communities such as the Tecuexe brought agaves in from the wild and selected clones and bulbils for propagation that grew well in open field settings. The second era of intense selection occurred during the last half of the nineteenth century. Today, cultivators have focussed all their attention on the blue agave clones, but they continue to select for uniformity in the dimensions of these plants. The mescaleros prefer working with the first vegetative offshoots emerging from the base of the mother plant, and they will even suspend disking and other means of weed control when offshoots start to emerge, in order to ensure that none are damaged.

How they treat the offshoots depends upon how much pressure there is on the mescaleros to save all offshoots for propagation in new plantations during periods of high demand. If demand is low relative to supply, the mescaleros quickly remove all offshoots that appear at the base of the mother plant; this total elimination of rhizomes is called *el tostoneo.* But there are two other options: *el desbote,* which refers to the removal of all offshoots that show evidence of disease or lack of vigor; and *el arranque,* which refers to the careful removal of healthy offshoots by severing their (underground) rhizomal connection to the mother plant, for transplanting into a nursery, and ultimately, into a new field. Obviously, el arranque is the choice that most mescaleros take during periods of short supply, such as the era we are in at the turn of the millennia (see appendix 1).

Are Traditional Practices Worth the Effort?

There is a prevailing opinion among older mescaleros that el tostoneo is ultimately of greatest benefit to the health and productivity of the mother plants, the generation of transplants reaching maturity. This rather severe pruning of vegetative offshoots, some agronomists have observed, risks damaging not only the offshoots but the mother plants as well, either through accidental cuts that injure the root masses, or through subsequent infection by pathogens.

In 1987, one of us (Ana) attempted to evaluate the benefits of el tostoneo as opposed to those of adding rooting hormones to mitigate the effects of any inadvertent damage. The results were curious because they suggested that the use of rooting hormones in the field hardly affected the production of new roots; whereas, the severity of tostoneo pruning reduced the production of roots by more than half the total dry weight of the root mass (Valenzuela-Zapata 1997). Why on earth, we wondered, did the older mescaleros insist on el tostoneo if this initial agronomic evaluation indicated that it was such an undesirable practice?

Several years passed before we could figure out why they insisted on such dramatic pruning. Why, we wondered, would a traditional practice persist more than a century if its premise was mistaken, and its damage to the plants significant? We had been so focused on the damage of potentially useful offshoots that we had not taken into account other factors. For instance, el tostoneo aided in the detection of diseases that had already infected the mother plant—by severely pruning the rhizomes, it was easy to see diseases such as *Fusarium* wilts infesting the plant's basal tissues. The risk of losing the mother plant to disease is far more costly than losing the initial batch of offshoots emerging from her base. In this sense, el tostoneo serves as a form of preventative medicine, providing mescaleros with early warning indicators that a disease is infecting their plantation. If the mother plant's health can be maintained and major infection averted, other offshoots can be obtained. Without a doubt, el tostoneo remains an important bet-hedging strategy, well worth the labor invested in it.

A similar case reaffirming the value of traditional practices involves another kind of pruning. This controversial practice is called *el barbeo* or "the barber's trim" by the mescaleros of the *zona centro* around Tequila. While some plantation owners argue that their workers waste too much time doing one kind of pruning after another, the older mescaleros insist that "the plants ask for it!" At first, we wondered, who is the better judge, fieldworkers, land owners, or agronomists?

It is clear that el barbeo prunings have been part of the annual cycle of agave-culture for well over a century, and that older mescaleros devote much of each June and July to accomplishing this work. It is especially necessary in smaller, unmechanized plantations, as well as in those where legume intercropping requires access between rows of agaves. Trimming the sharp terminal spines off the leaves clearly reduces the risk of workers getting stuck by these needle-like protrusions, but there are other cases where the benefits of trimming are not as obvious. For example, *el barbeo de escobeta* is only done on mature monocropped agaves, whether their fields are worked by hand labor or tractors. This pruning occurs late in the plant's life cycle, but nevertheless reduces its foliar biomass by half, thereby diminishing the plants' productivity in the final year prior to harvesting.

Why has such severe pruning become a time-honored practice among the mescaleros? When we asked them to explain their logic, they replied that they followed some simple guidelines: never prune in the winter, and only trim the plants back during periods of rapid growth when they can immediately compensate for any biomass lost. This is not only how and when they accomplish el barbeo de escobeta without setting the plant back, it is also how they evaluate the need for other prunings. The *cacheteo,* for example, is done only when workers completely lack access within and between rows. *El desemplague* is done strictly when there are fitosanitary problems that require removal of infected leaves. *El farol* and *el arbolito* are prunings performed only when plants need a shaping, while others are executed only on mature plants nearing harvest: *el barbeo castigado, barbeo de escobeta, banqueado, rebajado,* and *farol castigado* (Valenzuela-Zapata 1997).

Curiously, the traditional practices that Lázaro Pérez (1887) described in great detail for tending agave crops have persisted unchanged for more than a century. There is a rich body of traditional knowledge regarding the benefits of various kinds of pruning, and each is applied only under certain conditions and at certain times within the agave plant's life cycle. When we finally evaluated the effects of barbeo de escobeta, we found that pruning off the outer half of all leaves as well as the terminal leaf bud increased not only the photosynthetic activity of the remaining leaf area of the plants, but increased it per area of cultivated land as well. By comparing seven-year-old plants that had been frequently pruned with those that had never received pruning, we found that plants with pruned leaves had double the acidity per unit area during the night, and greater solar gain during the day. For a succulent that uses the Crassulacian Acid Metabolic (CAM) pathway to divide its photosynthetic process into light-gaining activities during the day and water-conserving activities during the night, doubling nocturnal acidity and increasing solar exposure are excellent strategies for increasing carbon gain while minimizing drought stress. The mescaleros recognize the same strategies in much simpler, more elegant terms: "by trimming off half the leaf mass in the barbeo de escobeta, we force the remaining ball [of leaves] to mature more rapidly."

The reductionist who sees everything as either good or bad, black or white, might ask, "Is pruning agaves good or bad for them?" "Neither good nor bad," we'd reply, for all depends upon when, how, and for whose purpose (the mother plant's, her vegetative offshoot's or "pup's," or the drunk waiting in the cantina for his next shooter).

Does Castration Make an Ox Out of an Agave?

There is one particular traditional plant management technique that is dying out even as we speak. It is the "castration" or removal of the *cogollo* (inflorescence scape) through a practice called *descogolle*. One day among many that we talked with elderly jimadores near Tequila, they told us that it was best to remove the scape before it is allowed to flower. Nevertheless, this practice is seldom seen in Tequila nowadays, even though it is commonly accomplished with wild agaves from the Zacatecas highlands all the way to the arid sierras in Sonora. This practice, as wild agave harvesters see it, keeps the plant from dissipating its energy in reproduction, allowing for more of its sugars to swell in the caudex and leaf bases prior to harvesting. However, in some wild agaves, it also encourages another flush of vegetative propagation by breaking apical dominance and promoting lateral shooting. This latter factor is not so important in cultivated fields (where some offshoots have already been spared to keep up the propagation of the clone) but it is of critical importance for the maintenance of wild populations. In fact, some elderly harvesters of wild agaves do not remove the mother plant until they are sure that offshoots have been produced. In addition, some elderly Sonorans have told us that they allow some of the resulting offshoots to flower in remote areas, rather than going back and harvesting them all. This practice, as once widely observed, had a positive effect on nectar-feeding bats and other pollinators of agaves, which seasonally depend on the availability of agave nectar to fuel their migration (Nabhan and Fleming 1993; Heacox 1989; Arita and Wilson 1989).

Unfortunately, the traditional knowledge and even the folk terminology for this practice is not only being lost among cultivators of blue agave. It is also being lost among wild harvesters of *mescal bacanora,* who annually remove as many as 1.2 million mature and immature rosettes of wild *Agave angustifolia* from the *zona serrana* of Sonora and adjacent states (Nabhan and Fleming 1993). Borewell (1995) has presumptuously asserted that all Sonoran mescaleros believe it is fruitless to quantify the regional pressures on agave resources—since they vary how many they harvest from year to year—but he makes a mistake in assuming that the nectar-feeding bats' dependence on agaves is always as loose as that of the thirty mescaleros he attempted to interview. Borewell also makes the tragic mistake of assuming that traditional harvesters and recently relocated novices in the Sonoran foothills have equal effects on the persistence of clones, and on the availability of agaves, as do future harvests of rosettes by mescaleros and nectar by bats.

It is remarkable that jimadores around Tequila still retain knowledge of the ancient and formerly widespread practice of descogolle. This demonstrates the complex of agronomic and ecological issues addressed by orally transmitted reservoirs of traditional knowledge, which, unfortunately, scientists misunderstand more often than they understand. There remain many parts of the agrarian tradition of the jimadores that have yet to be investigated, and there will be many surprises when this tradition is given proper attention. It is important to document the logic of traditional practices before they entirely disappear.

The Jima—A Sophisticated Harvesting Technique

There is one group of fieldworkers who never seem to take a rest—during rains or droughts—and they are known as the "jimadores." Their work is less seasonally shifting than that of other campesinos working in the agave plantations—there are agaves ready to harvest year-round. They must seek out the mature agaves, trim back all their leaves so that only an ovoid sphere remains, and remove these "heads" or "pineapples" from the fields. To accomplish this task, a man must grow expert in handling a coa de jima—a circular blade fifteen to twenty centimeters in diameter, sharply filed and attached to a wooden handle.

The men attracted to this single chore comprise a special group of workers, for the rigors of this work are not fully compensated for relative to the wages that other fieldworkers earn. The typical jimador is not necessarily taller or heavier or stronger than other laborers, but he has learned how to apply his energy and to exact the placement of his coa for maximum impact on the agaves.

A squadron of experienced jimadores is better coordinated than any other work crew we have ever seen. As they move through a plantation together, taking turns at dislodging and trimming a sequence of mature agaves, they harvest between three and four thousand kilograms of roastable agaves over six hours of steady work per day. In other words, each man transforms seventy-five to one hundred mature agaves into forty-kilogram "pineapples" during the 360 minutes he has his coa de jima in hand each day. That amounts to digging up, dislodging, severing, and trimming each mature agave in 3.6 to 4.8 minutes. More than one hundred leaves are trimmed back to their bases before the head is ready to carry over to the nearest truck parked on the field edge.

The jimadores may return to the same plantation over four consecutive years, since not all of the agaves planted at the same time mature simultaneously. During the first year of harvest, they seldom remove more than 15 percent of the maturing plants. During the second and third years of harvest, the jimadores attempt to remove about 30 percent of the total population annually, and by the fourth year, less than 20 percent of the total planting remains to be harvested.

Nevertheless, the percentages, the estimates of efficiency, the total weights of the harvest, hardly tell the story as well as simply watching a seasoned jimador work over a plant in less than five minute's time from start to finish. He refiles his blade, selects which plant is mature, then hurls the coa toward one leaf base after another with astounding precision. When the jimador brings his metal blade down on the succulent leaf of blue agave, you can hear a *jjim* with every cut—not unlike the sound of El Zorro's sword—then the sigh that follows. Perhaps that's why they call the harvest *"jjimaa."*

Out of the Fields, into the Fire

Tradition and Globalization

ᒧ ᒧ ᒧ

The farmers have somehow preserved a style of family-based production, one which does not stand in the way of what has also become a large-scale agro-industry; they continue to use traditional cultivation practices at the same time they try to find appropriate roles for advances from biotechnology; they appreciate home-selected seeds, but are aggressively entering the international marketplace. The rural plurality of Mexico does not easily fall apart in the intermingling of tradition and modernity.
—Armando Batra, *Mitos Mexicanos*

A Funny Thing Happened on the Way to the Airline Terminal

We are walking around the Guadalajara International Airport, and in its duty-free shopping area, most of the shops appear familiar to us—they have the same mix of sundries, magazines, watches, and paraphernalia for cameras that we've seen in airports in other cities, on other continents. But then we encounter a shop that is an anomaly, one that hardly seems to fit among the *PC World* and *Cosmopolitan* magazines stacked up in the corner of the adjacent newsstand.

A videotape is showing blue-green landscapes filled with thousands of agaves, where lean men in sombreros are trimming back each mature plant into the form of a blue pineapple. On shelves below the video monitor, there are bottles with four different colored labels, each designating a different aging process for the

100-percent-agave alcohols that they hold. Surrounding the colorful bottles are leather jackets and vests, blue jean vests and shirts, caps, and wallets all carrying the insignia of a distillery. Calendars, shot glasses, and pamphlets carry the distillery's logo, but they might be the very same items found with the Jack Daniel's logo on them in shops of the Deep South, or with the logo of a Napa Valley winery in California. Nevertheless, amidst all the bustle and urbanity of the airport, they speak a singular language of rural nostalgia to most of the visitors who walk in the door of the shop. They speak of the country life, the charismatic charros, and the Tapatio tradition. Here in the midst of Mexico's second largest metropolitan area, which now heralds itself as the Silicon Valley of Latin America, we are suddenly tasting and smelling the fragrance of the countryside, not of the city. We breathe it in, purchase a moment of tranquility, then slide back into a lane of traffic headed for God-knows-where.

Keeping a Stall in the Global Marketplace

Tequila has traveled to all parts of the world and has even received the recognition of the European Union, with its acceptance of tequila's Denomination of Origin, signed in 1997. Perhaps that agreement was the most significant for tequila in achieving international status as a unique product that should be free of adulteration, for Europe is the continent where the Denominations of Origin for champagne, cognac, scotch, and many wines have long been honored. From its first burst into the international marketplace, tequila has always been given an impressive amount of attention, heralded as a spirit altogether distinctive.

After three centuries of distilling the sugary juices of agaves, the tequila tradition has shed some its former elements and revived others that had nearly atrophied. It has renewed its commitment to 100-percent-agave sugars when that has proved advantageous, and it has learned how to honor its history in labeling and advertising. Nevertheless, its actors are not exclusively *tapatíos*, or old Jaliscan families; distilleries and distributors are now directed by absentee owners from Mexico City, London, Los Angeles, and New York.

The evolution of the tequila-making business has varied in

rate and in scale, and the only way to characterize the spectrum of players is to refer to their absolute heterogeneity. While the number of distilleries more than doubled to seventy between 1995 and 2000, some are micro-distillery custom houses; others are medium-sized, family-based legacies; and still others are branches of large multinational corporations involved in producing, distributing, and retailing alcohol worldwide. The older firms, which have been exporting tequila for more than a century, have somehow been converted into huge corporations without losing their folksy identity. With the recent creation of the Consejo Regulador del Tequila (CRT), there is now momentum to integrate all phases of the industry to improve overall product quality and plan for periods of surplus and scarcity.

Tequila making has somehow become an industry characterized by a spirit of coexistence. It accommodates the large and the small; the ancient and the new; those of the core area around Tequila as well as those of Los Altos and of adjacent states; and both the specialized tequileros and the mescal-making generalists.

These relationships are nested in strategic alliances with the giants of the distribution and commercialization of alcoholic beverages, for without outside investment and a many-tentacled infrastructure, it would be difficult to retain a place in the global marketplace. All who are covered under this umbrella strategy retain the absolute competitive advantage: they are promoting a tradition-rich unique product that has global name recognition and distribution. Tequila has positively changed its image from that of a generic distillate, good for a cheap drunk. And, of course, it has been graced by its rather mysterious origins, a colorful history, a rustic if not picturesque means of cultivation and elaboration, and a cultural and ecological context that gives it special meaning. Somehow its aficionados have come to realize that each drink of *tequila añejo* is not merely a fleeting pleasure; it has been heightened by eight years of nurturing by many hands!

Tradition and Contemporaneity

The time-honored procedure for elaborating tequila begins, as does all processing of mescal for food or for drink, with the baking of agaves in roasting pits. In Jalisco, the roasting pits were traditionally shaped as inverted truncated cones, which first accommodate bonfires of firewood, then agaves, then a cap of stones (Pérez 1887). Over the burning coals, the trimmed heads of agave are fit into the pit and then covered with grass, burlap, moistened earth, or flagstones, leaving a small central ventilation hole through which the heat can be monitored and water can be applied (Villalvazo-Rodriquez 1986; Luna-Zamora 1991).

Of course, there are many regional variations in the pit-roasting, depending upon the materials used for fuelwood, the texture and depth of the soil around the pit, the size and quantity of heads, and the availability of materials for sealing the pit shut (Castetter et al. 1938). After one-and-a-half to three days of pit-roasting, the baked, caramelized heads are mashed in a *molino Chileno* (Chilean mill) also known as *tahona* or *ta'una*. This mill is composed of two gigantic circular grindstones fitted atop one another, with the upper stone of four tons attached to a central spindle-shaft or axle. The mill is driven by the circling of a draft horse, mule, or burro spurred on by a muleskinner's whips and whistles. By the middle of the 1800s, these volcanic grindstones were being replaced by sugar cane pressing mills called *trapiches.*

The mashed agaves and their juices are transported by bucket from the grindstones to tanks, where other workers break up large chunks to establish a filtered slurry suitable for even fermentation of the sugars. Today, such tanks are no longer made of wood or fired earth; late in the nineteenth century, the more rustic tanks were replaced with carefully sealed masonry vats (Luna-Zamora 1991). The internationalization of tequila, crowned by the "brandy awards" given to the Sauza family's mescals at the Chicago World's Fair in 1893, ushered in this upscaling of fermentation and distillation technologies.

In the 1970s, fermentation technology took another turn, into the antiseptic world of stainless-steel autoclaves regulated by temperature gauges. These receptacles function as gigantic pressure-cookers, in which water vapor is injected to stimulate steam-baking. Ironically, such precision-based baking technologies have not entirely replaced the other two historically prevalent methods; each tequila firm selects a mix of ancient and modern technologies to fit its image as well as its scale of production.

Whatever the method, the objective is to extract the sugary juices of the mescal plant, converting their complex carbohydrates from starchy polysaccharides to simple, more easily digestible sugars. These sugars can then be metabolized by yeasts to obtain a fermented alcoholic beverage. What steam-baking or pit-roasting does is quite simple—it hydrolyzes the slowly digestible inulin starches found in the heart or caudex of an agave, converting them to fermentable fructoses and sucroses. Ironically, the further this conversion proceeds, the less value the inulin starches have as "slow release" food capable of controlling blood sugar levels in sufferers of diabetes. To this day, Germany and Switzerland import partially baked, inulin-rich agave pulp from Mexico to serve as a slow-release carbohydrate in specialty dietetic foods for diabetics. Once the fermenting is done, however, the imbibing of alcohols derived from agave sugars can send genetically vulnerable non-insulin dependent diabetes mellitus (NIDDM) sufferers into a diabetic coma.

In the end, the agave has yielded most of its simple sugars to be used in the fermentation process, while the remaining bagasse is filtered out for use as a combustible or as a field mulch. The slurry of juices is then siphoned away, and at least for the 51 percent agave tequilas allowable by law, mixed with other sugars. Cane sugar is the most commonly added ingredient, and it is carefully combined with agave sugars in the processing stage called "sugar formulation." Of course, tequila produced from 100 percent agave requires no such formulation stage, and the *mostos* (fermentable agave sugars) for these products are passed directly into the fermentation stage.

There's Something Alive in Your Drink

Through fermentation, which is at the very base of the industrial process, the agave sugars are transformed into ethyl alcohol, as well as other by-products of minor proportions (Villalvazo-Rodriquez 1986). Historically, mescal was fermented in wooden casks then carried through the distillation process in rustic clay pots and copper coil stills. Today, fermentation is completed in enormous twenty-thousand-liter stainless-steel tanks, where the mescal sugars, water, and yeasts are mixed in the exact proportions determined to be optimal by each tequila firm. The duration of fermentation varies with season, since temperature and humidity are key factors driving the process, but it can take up to six days. Some processors claim that under the cooler temperatures of winter months, fermentation takes an additional twenty-four hours. The process is not unlike those mediated by other microorganisms; first there is exponential growth in yeast activity, then there is a second phase where effervescence reach a plateau, and finally there is a decline in yeast activity as other microbes enter the scene.

The principal actors in any live event of fermentation include alcohol, carbon dioxide, water, and energy released in the form of heat. The mescal wine or crude liquor produced by full fermentation is effervescent, but its bubbling ceases when the yeasts terminate their life's work. The brewers in the distillery carefully watch for the final moment of life among the beer yeasts, knowing that at last they have converted all available mescal sugars to alcohol. The once murky, bubbly brown brew lies still (Hutson 1995).

The fermented mescal is now ready to put into stainless-steel boilers for distillation, passing the heated vapor up a tubular column or *capitel*, which collects and transports the vapor into the copper coil or *serpentín*, where the vapor is cooled until it condenses into a distilled liquid. With the two distillations, the spirits of the fermented brew are separated from everything else by way of temperature and pressure, yielding products rich in alcohol (vino-mescal de tequila) and in vinegar precursors *(vinazas)*; the latter are usually thrown away. It is possible, however, to further process the vinegar precursors, known locally as *lodos de fermentación* or "fermentation dregs," after giving them more water and yeast. Usable vinegars are the result.

The different boiling points of various compounds and their varied volumes, along with the varying pressure build-up in the still at different times, all aid in the separation of gases, each of which condenses to add to the richness in flavor of the tequila during the first run of distillation. However, two passes through the still are needed, the first called the *destrozamiento* or "havoc-making," for it produces a sequence of wildly different strengths: the *cabeza* or "head," the *corazón* or "heart," and the *cola* or "tail."

When accumulated together, these three components of the first distillation are called *tequila ordinario,* and average 38–40 proof. Only the heart is saved for the second distillation, since the head and tail are loaded with impurities such as fusel oils, methanol, and ethanol (Hutson 1995). The second distillation is called the *rectificación,* which after filtration results in a 110 proof product. During the rectificación, the richness of alcohol increases and all impurities are eliminated, so that the final run is of highest quality. The tequila produced by the second, rectifying pass is known as *tequila blanco.*

A Taxonomy of Tequilas

The fundamental dichotomy that separates kinds of tequila distinguishes between those made of 100-percent-agave sugars and the *mixtos,* which mix sugar cane and other sweeteners with agave sugars. The mixtos were formerly allowed to have up to 49 percent of their sugars from other sources, but now industry standards allow for no more than 40 percent of the sugars to be derivative of other plants (Sánchez-Lacy 1998). For a tequila to be labeled as a 100-percent-agave product, it must jump through several hoops: bottling must be done in the same place as distillation so that the exclusive use of agave sugars can be verified, and that place must fall within the areas of the official *zona tequilera.* That zone is defined as those municipalities in Jalisco, Nayarit, Guanajato, Michoacán, and Tamaulipas that are authorized by the Denomination of Origin published in Mexico's Federal Register, the *Diario Oficial.*

The Mexican government norms do allow for certain additives to be used to soften and smooth the taste of any tequila: caramel coloring, oak wood extracts, glycerin, as well as (corn) sugar syrups. The tequilas processed with such additives are called *abocados,* implying that their flavor has been softened, sweetened, or enhanced through aging, seasoning, or decanting in certain vessels. The abocados are juxtaposed with the blancos, which receive no aging in oak barrels, nor any coloring by additives. Even the process of aging or maturation of tequilas is legally defined by SECOFI, Mexico's Secretary of Commerce: "[It is] the slow transformation that permits the product to acquire certain desirable organoleptic characteristics through chemical processes that occur naturally during a period of storage in oak barrels" (1994).

The Mexican government's norms then proceed to set out a typology for four distinct kinds of tequila (Sánchez-Lacy 1998; Hutson 1995):

Tequila blanco or *tequila plata*—white or silver. Blancos are clear as water, and are the direct, unadulterated products of the second distillation. The alcohol content of blancos can, however, be diluted by the addition of demineralized water. Unblended, they are often intense in their somewhat smokey, almost peppery aroma, nearly overwhelming any hints of herbal, citric, and fruity aftertastes. The more coarsely distilled blancos feel as though they can burn your lips, and have an oily, petrol aftertaste, but others are sweet and earthy. They are the classic tequilas used in margaritas and fruit drinks or served straight-up on ice.

Tequila joven or *tequila oro*—gold. Oros can be colored or flavored by caramels, or seasoned a few months in oak barrels to mellow their flavor. They can also be diluted by water, or their appearance adjusted in other ways by additives. Blancos, when mixed with *añejos* or *reposados,* can be labeled as oros. Many so-called oros reaching the United States are mixtos, rather than 100-percent-agave products. These tequilas are more popular in the United States than in Mexico, and are used in margaritas and mixed drinks. They are also downed as "shooters."

Tequila reposado—aged. Reposados can be enhanced by additives and by aging, but the "resting" in oak or pine barrels must last at least two months. The first reposado ever marketed was from Herradura, and it was aged fourteen months in order to gain a balance between the tannins in the oak barrels and the richness of the agave sugars. Sometimes reposados of different ages are blended, and the average period of seasoning in oak barrels for all components is the age listed on the label, weighted by the relative volumes of all components. Reposados carry with them various woody, vanilla, and herbal aftertastes, but never lose the aroma of agaves. If anything, the fragrance of agaves is so enhanced that reposados are best sipped rather than mixed into cocktails. They have become the most widely imbibed tequilas, known for their lovely straw and tawny colors.

Tequila añejo—extra-aged. Although additives can be used, the primary characteristic of añejo tequilas is their aging in small oak barrels for a minimum of twelve months. Even their alcohol content can be adjusted by dilution with demineralized water. Like blended reposados, the age listed for blended añejos is the average age of all components, weighted by the relative contribution by volume. They vary wildly in their quality, from mellow, fruity cognac-like flavors, to astringent, tannin-heavy grappa-like tastes. The marketplace has found room for tequilas that have been aged two, three, five, or ten years, and no doubt someone is hiding away twenty-year-old tequilas, which will be darker and even richer in their tannin-rich woodsiness.

The New Tequilas

The image of tequila today is that of a beverage for sophisticates, one elaborated with care by the stewards of an ancient tradition. The jargon of California's wine-tasters has now intruded upon the banter of tequila's aficionados. They will describe a newly released añejo as being "full-bodied, with a hint of tropical fruits, cedar, and fresh flowers, rich in texture, smooth, with an aftertaste both sweet and fragrant." Or they will speak of another as exhibiting "a singularly smooth and velvety flavor with a somewhat woody tone, heightened by four years of aging in white oak barrels." Some will claim that not a single additive is allowed, while others focus on the style and scale of roasting, fermenting, and distilling (Sánchez-Lacy 1998).

The new tequilas that have overtaken the international marketplace lure their drinkers with handblown glass containers or ceramic vessels designed by Jaliscan craftsmen. Some are boxed in wooden barrels, chests, and carrying cases; others are slung into animal-hide canteens. One of the tequilas from northern Jalisco, Porfidio, has a multiarmed columnar cactus of glass blown into the base of its bottle. Some have labels made from *amate* fiber, designed to look just as the pre-Columbian codices first appeared to the Conquistadors; others celebrate the ravens, iguanas, horses, and deer that once frequented the countryside of Nueva Galicia (Sánchez-Lacy 1998).

Today, not only the use of 100 percent agave and the duration of aging grace the labels; advertising that the product is from "Los Altos" (and not from the central zone around the town of Tequila) now means something to connoisseurs. Even though there are only seventy distilleries, they produce more than four hundred distinct products among the four tequila types and their derivative aperitifs, elixirs, and liqueurs. As unbelievable as it seems for those of us who purchased our first bottle of tequila for less than five dollars, the premiums and supreme selections now garner up to two thousand dollars per bottle, and seventy dollars per glass. The dicho or folk saying that tequilas are here to help us *quitar las penas* (take away our worries) does not seem to work well with these high-end brands. Those who drink them have few worries, at least financial, to begin with, or they drink despite their many worries, and the evening's bar bill will bring them a few more.

The Amatitán Valley of Jalisco is likely the most ancient area of origin for cultivation of tequila's ancestors and there, tequila producers retain a rich oral tradition. The volcanic features of this stunning landscape have generated red soils that have supported agave cultivation for upwards of four centuries.

Vegetative offshoots are used as "seeds" (propagules) for an agave crop. A traditional system of agave management has developed in the cultural communities in the central valleys of Jalisco. For the last three centuries, the lines have been regenerated by clonal propagation.

During the summer, agaves are often intercropped in the Tequila region with legumes, maize, and squashes. Garbanzos are also used as autumn-winter intercrops with young agaves. Unfortunately, these polycultures are being replaced by the monocultures favored by large-scale producers.

The *azul* cultivar produces few fertile seeds, so propagation occurs by transplanting bulbils produced on inflorescences that fail to receive cross-pollination. After the flowers wither, bulbils emerge from the bracteole meristem and are photosynthetically dependent on the mother plant until rooted.

The appearance of flowering agaves—such as these at Rancho El Indio in Jalisco—is rare in cultivated fields. This is because the flowering cycle of the plants must be inhibited by pruning back the emerging *quiote* (inflorescence) in order to produce harvestable plants with the greatest inulin storage in their basal meristematic tissues.

Agave harvesters, known as *jimadores* (from *jima*, to prune or to cut), are trained by their families in the traditional ecological knowledge of plant management. Once trained, they can typically uproot, trim, and prepare for roasting a mature agave in a matter of six minutes. To do so, the *jimador* must always maintain a razor-sharp edge on his *coa de jima* tool and must quickly assess the quality and position of each agave.

Here an agave distillery worker is accomplishing the final preparation of the *cabeza* (head) or *piña* (pineapple) for baking in a steam oven. He removes any young leaves or woody tissues that might produce a bitter taste in the final product. The harvested plant's inulin starches are now ready to be converted by heat into flavorful sugars.

This pile of agave cabezas (heads) came from plants that matured six to twelve months in the field following the pruning of their quiotes (inflorescences). This maturation period is essential for the making of the best distilled mescals, since it allows the inulins and secondary flavor compounds to accumulate in the plant.

The agaves have been placed in the steam oven behind this wooden door; the small square window is used to check on the completeness of the baking process.

Once removed from the oven, the baked cabezas (heads) are put on conveyor belts and run through machines that help separate the fibrous pulp, or *bagazo* (bagasse) from the sugars, which will be fermented in wooden vats.

The sugary pulp and juices are filtered and then put into fermentation tanks with brewer's yeast. When cane sugar is added to this mix before the temperature is increased to hasten the fermentation process, these products cannot be labeled as "100% agave."

Two phases of distillation, the *destrozamiento* (separation from solids) and the final *rectificación* (rectification), are required to produce tequila. During each phase, distillers measure the alcohol and methanol content of the product to ensure that they fall within the percentages required by law.

Tequila reposado (tequila in repose) is aged in oak barrels to "soften" its flavors; the aging process adds oak tanning to the distillate, giving them a distinctive amber hue.

Today, large stainless steel vats are used to store tequila until it is bottled. A regulatory commission ensures that the tequilas bottled in Jalisco are labeled according to the ways they have been produced (with or without cane sugar additives) and aged.

In the center of origin for tequila production in Jalisco, natural history and cultural history intertwine to form the rich and elegant legacy of *mezcal de Tequila*. Here we see agave heads ready for distillation.

When the Epidemic Hit the
King of Clones

◆ ◆ ◆

It is an old story remembered in the Zapata family, known by all
of Ana's kin. When her older brother came home drunk, Lupe
Zapata ran to hide amidst the corrals behind their house. She
didn't hide for fear as much as for the pain it gave her to see her
brother in such a drunken condition. She then swore to God:
"Lord, bring some plague to dry up all the agaves, to rid us of all
this [drunkenness]!" Sixty years after she cast her spell, that plague
has come, reshaping the trajectory of the tequila industry as dramatically as any factor has within our lifetimes.

In 1988 we began to hear rumors from agave producers, rumors about a plague—based on several crop pathogens—more aggressive than anything they had previously witnessed. From that
time on, we began to observe a blight that made one agave leaf
after another turn yellow, encircled with rust-toned bands the
mescaleros called "el anillo rojo" (Rosen 1995; Nabhan 1997). In
some plants, the leaves would lose both their sky-blue intensity
and their rigidity; they would roll up, and split open and ooze below the terminal spine, probably as the result of another pathogen
(Romero 1998). The putrefying remains of the dying plants were
not unlike those suffering from a known fungal infection that occasionally affected stressed agaves, but the damage did not seem to
be from a single cause.

When the plague came to the attention of our old friend
Guadalupe Fonseca, who directs all fieldwork for one of the major agribusinesses in the region, he commented that it seemed as
though plagues always arrive in the best times, when weather and

business are favorable. We had all heard of the "gangrene" that agaves suffered during the first tequila boom a century before. And our colleagues in Oaxaca, Claudia López and Felipe Cruz, had been shown other analogous diseases there by local magueyeros just four years earlier. From that time on, we saw such infestations advance from one field to the next until it was evident in one fifth of all agaves planted in Jalisco, damaging nearly forty million plants in 1998 alone (Romero 1998). From Oaxaca to Nayarit, there was a plague upon the land.

Becoming Botanical Detectives

What we saw was exactly what other researchers had begun to document: a rotting of agave flesh caused perhaps by fungus infesting the stalks, caudex, and base of the plant. These fungal pathogens ruthlessly attacked the *cogollo,* or terminal growth bud. The fungus behaved as though it were a strain of *Fusarium,* a cause of wilt in many crops. But we also recognized that there was another element to the putrefaction, not unlike the symptoms seen during the last major agave disease outbreak. That epidemic had been caused by a bacterial stem rot known as *secazón* (the big withering). That round of damage was blamed on the bad guys known as *Erwinia,* a number of strains of bacterial pathogens found to wreak havoc on both wild and cultivated plant tissues. *Erwinia* bacteria often infect plants that are already stressed by freezes, drought, winds, or excessive heat, but they also do time after the plants have died, speeding up tissue decay as part of the recycling crew.

Regardless how many pathogens were involved, there was something about this epidemic that was vaguely reminiscent of the plague that devastated agave crops during the first tequila boom of the nineteenth century. Curiously, in both cases, the epidemics occurred not long after a large quantity of vegetative offshoots were planted in monocultural stands on extensive acreages, in response to meteoric rises in tequila demand. We were of course aware of the theoretical risks associated with any monoculture, but we quickly realized that the even age of the transplanted clonal offshoots was also an aggravating factor. If the vast majority of agaves out in the fields were of just one age class, then their enemies—as well as their natural allies, perhaps—would have a field day. The problem was one of demographic vulnerability—two-thirds of the two hundred million agaves growing in Jalisco were planted within just a couple years of one another, all derived from the same clone, blue agave.

That bit of news meant that all the eggs had indeed been put in one basket. Under such circumstances, how could there be any capacity at all to be buffered genetically from an epidemic? This genetic vulnerability, which we first predicted several years before tragedy struck (Valenzuela-Zapata 1995; Nabhan 1985, 1997), has recently been confirmed by scientist Benjamín Rodríguez Garay, who explained it to science reporter Laura Romero (1998): "The tequila agave casts its blue color on sixty thousand hectares of hills and valleys where not a single other kind of agave is allowed a foot-hold, and its means of propagation by cloning in such large quantities has caused a grave problem for the crop—that of genetic uniformity."

Although some cryptic somaclonal variants with disease resistance might occur within the two hundred million offshoots set out in the countryside, this kind of genetic variation has hardly been studied and would have been hard to mobilize in time to fend off the epidemic. Worse yet, the semidomesticated progenitors and relatives of the blue agave clone have been virtually outlawed by the industry, and could hardly be located for resistance screening. The blue landscape that has been packed so full of agaves is now withering, threatened by its very success.

How can further losses be averted? How might health return to the land of tequila? How can we respond to the "economic disaster" that has already affected the thirty-five thousand families that rely on tequila production for their primary means of livelihood?

Return to Intercropping

Regardless of the level of genetic uniformity among the agaves themselves, there is less disease in virtually all tequila plantations that intersperse rows of peanuts or green beans between rows of agaves. These ground-covering, nitrogen-fixing legumes suppress the weeds that serve as vectors for diseases, and improve the soil.

Ironically, the industry has discouraged intercropping over the last thirty years, considering it less efficient than agave monoculture as a use of arable lands suited to tequila cultivation. With the agave-culture tradition, intercropping was the rule, not the exception. Several of our own field studies (Valenzuela-Zapata 1992, 1995; Nelson, Nabhan, and Robichaux 1991) have demonstrated the advantages, as well as the limitations, of intercropping agaves or other monocots with legumes.

Returning to Spatial Mixtures of Different Agave Varieties

It has been convincingly demonstrated, theoretically as well as in the field, that mixing resistant and susceptible varieties of a monocot crop in the same field, or in adjacent fields, slows down the spread and virulence of diseases and pests (Gould 1986). In the case of the tequila-growing area of Jalisco, there was no doubt a mix of fiber and beverage agaves grown in the same area up until the time of the first boom, when blue agave clones were selected for their short maturation cycle (Perez 1887). Since that time, several of the cultivated varieties with very distinct fiber characteristics and rosette architectures have been lost from the landscape as plantings of significant scale (Valenzuela-Zapata 1995; Franco-Martínez 1995). However, several of these nearly extinct land races or heirloom varieties, including *zopilote* and *pata de mula*, have been recently rediscovered and given taxonomic rank in this volume.

These materials should be among the highest priorities for conservation *in situ* and *ex situ*, as well as for inclusion in agroecological experiments undertaken to solve current problems (Franco-Martínez 1995). Studies of their leaf morphology, fiber anatomy, pollen, and stomata are now underway at the Universidad de Guadalajara. At the Jardin Botanico de la UNAM and the Centro de Investigación y Asistencia en Tecnología y Diseño del Estado de Jalisco (CIATEJ), micropropagules of these cultivated varieties, as well as other agave species, are being screened for disease resistance to the bacterial and fungal pathogens implicated in the red ring epidemic (Romero 1998). Those that have resistance can be regenerated through somatic embryogenesis in less than six months, and then rapidly multiplied by other tissue culture techniques. However, rather than planting a single resistant selection on large acreages, it would still be more prudent to plant intermixtures of various agave varieties to slow down the evolution of virulence in the fungal and bacterial pathogens (Gould 1986). To achieve such a mosaic of plantings of various agave varieties, the industry would need to reconsider its exclusive use of the azul cultivar, and allow other varieties to be used in tequila production, just as it did a few decades ago.

Returning to Cross-Pollinated Agave Crops

Although many agaves are capable of vegetative propagation as well as sexual reproduction, few blue agave plants are ever allowed to flower, thus nectar-feeding bats and other floral visitors are unable to cross-pollinate them with pollen from nearby wild or cultivated plants. Bats such as the *murcielago magueyero (Leptonycteris curasoae)* have historically been responsible for the diversification of certain agave lineages, including that of *Agave angustifolia* (Arita and Martinez del Rio 1988). Cross-pollination often fosters genetic recombination in agaves, fueling the process of reticulate evolution that has allowed agaves to adapt to new abiotic stresses and to biotic challenges from pests and pathogens (Gentry 1982).

Over the long run, cross-pollination by bats or by human plant breeders will probably be necessary to keep the domesticated species of agaves evolving in response to new anthropogenic environments and stresses (Hernandez-Xolocotzi 1993). However, it is doubtful whether allowing some tequila agaves to flower will produce the needed results in time to slow down the current epidemic. It will, however, recruit and sustain populations of now-declining bats that are responsible for pollinating a number of agave species along a fifteen-hundred-kilometer nectar corridor between Jalisco and the U.S.–Mexico borderlands. Restoring the relationship between bats and paniculate agaves makes good sense for agave germ plasm conservation in general (Franco-Martínez 1995; Nabhan and Fleming 1993), even if it does not immediately aid tequila growers.

Effects of the Economic Cycle on Agaves

The very fact that agaves have a long life cycle affects disease control strategies in many ways. Just as other crops are influenced by commodity price fluctuations, so are tequila crops, but in peculiar ways. Prices may fluctuate several times over the life span of a multi-annual crop like that of blue agave, which may take as much as twelve years to complete its entire life cycle. A good price at the time of harvest stimulates the expansion of plantings and the demand for farmworkers. But if prices plummet due to declines in demand or to over-production, investments in the management and care of immature crops are reduced. Plantation managers pay laborers less to keep the agaves free of weeds, so pests and diseases are more likely to spread. When the *sobreoferta* or "excess supply" peaked between 1993 and 1998, some plantations were abandoned, left to die or to be overrun by weeds.

There are many adverse effects of these fluctuations on the regional economy. When prices are high, land owners wish to pack as many agaves onto their fields as possible, so that monoculture is favored over intercropping. As prices decline, the industry lacks the extra resources to establish intercrops on available parcels. There are similar effects on the quality and diversity of vegetative offshoots used for plantings. When prices are high, the demand for vegetatively propagated plantlets is also high, so that the clones that are most prolific are used to establish more plantations, regardless of their susceptibility to stresses. Poor quality offshoots get planted simply because demand creates a relative scarcity of carefully selected propagules. When prices drop, there is hardly any pressure to select only the highest quality propagules, because hardly anyone is planting at that time anyway.

In this manner, the economic cycle actually heightens the region's vulnerability to infestations by fungal and bacterial pathogens. In the early 1990s, prices for blue agave began to decline, and so the manpower dedicated to weeding and removing sick agaves from fields was diminished. Many fields were abandoned altogether, leaving a young cohort of plants on the land without plans for harvesting them. There were few incentives for investing in intercropping or seasonal grazing between rows, because the densest monocultures remained the most cost-efficient fields for harvesting. But these fields then became infested with pathogens that swept through, moving from plant to plant with utter ease. Meanwhile, the clone, in all its splendor of genetic uniformity, lacks the capacity to coevolve with the pathogens in a way that allows resistant clonal variants to persist.

As the 1990s came and went, the period of sobreoferta was followed by a shortfall of agaves relative to the global demand. Wildcat harvesters formed clandestine crews that entered abandoned fields at night, removing any agaves that were reaching maturity. Prices for *materia prima* tripled, since diseases had decimated even the most well-kempt plantations. For the first time in thirty years, some tequila firms' annual budgets were running in the red; their production costs had suddenly gone through the roof. There were twice as many distilleries as five years earlier, so that profits from the ever-rising demand for tequila were divided among many niche markets. To no one's surprise, investments in advertising and marketing reached an all-time high, as many of the older firms had to peddle harder simply to stay in place.

It is hoped that the CRIT can help reduce the viciousness of such cycles, smoothing out the ups and downs of supply and demand. The trouble that remains is one of education: few economic botanists ever come to understand the economic cycles of agro-industries, and few agricultural economists ever come to understand how the life cycles of plants affect the dynamics that they study. Although the life span of an agave is long relative to the amount of time it takes for agave aficionados to obtain their undergraduate and graduate degrees, this dilemma is unlikely to be resolved within just one generation of professional development. The agaves are there, in the fields, waiting for us to get wise enough to help them out of this mess.

Landscape and Pueblo

Putting Tequila in Place

▲ ▲ ▲

Less than 12 miles east of Magdalena [Jalisco] is Tequila, set amid the spiky fields of maguey. Like Tecate [in Baja California Norte], it is as much a product as a place; more than 50 distilleries supply the world with tequila. Though the town was founded in 1530 by Cristobál de Oñate, it wasn't until 1873 that Don Cenobio Sauza laid the foundation for the modern tequila industry there.

—Charles Kulander, *West México: From Sea to Sierra*

Under the Volcano

Tequila, Jalisco, lies in a volcanic landscape where lava once flowed, just as mescal flows there today. You need not walk far from town before encountering the pyroclastic stone that Tecuexe Indians used to fashion their agave knives. Obsidian, the old-timers in the cantinas claim, was called "tequila" in some ancient indigenous dialect no longer spoken in the valley (Martínez-Limón 1998). Regardless of its ultimate origins, the word "tequila," they say, was also once used for "any stone that cuts." They liken mescal de Tequila to an obsidian knife in the way it cuts through the phlegm of life.

As of the last census, there were between twenty-five thousand and fifty thousand hectares of rocky, volcanic soils on which the blue tequila agave was grown in Jalisco (INEGI 1997). Nearly 95 percent of the two hundred million tequila plants grown within the volcanic area blessed by the Denomination of Origin are found in just ten small Jaliscan municipalities (Valenzuela-Zapata 1997). In 1901, these lands produced only nine and a half million liters of tequila. By 1980, they were producing nearly seventy million liters per year, of which 57 percent was consumed by Mexican drinkers (Raminez-Rancano 1999). Mexicans, on average, now drink one third more tequila than they drank in 1901, when 87 percent of all alcohol consumed in Mexico was in the form of the more ancient but less intoxicating agave beverage, pulque. Whereas pulque is only 4.25 percent alcohol, tequilas range from 38 percent to 43 percent alcohol. This change in Mexican patterns of alcohol consumption may have something to do with the estimate that by 1997, forty-eight million Mexicans drank heavily enough to be considered addicts (Raminez-Rancano 1999).

As the thirst for tequila became unquenchable after 1985, the flame that fuels this fire spread from fertile valleys and undulating plains to the steeper more unforgiving barrancas of Jalisco and adjacent states. It has run down steeper slopes, onto poorer, rockier soils, but has not stopped moving. Nevertheless, the heart of tequila production remains the same, located between 20° and 21° N, 102° and 104° W, where the volcanically derived obsidian chips still catch the tropical sun and shine like pieces of glass from a broken bottle of mescal. This tequila heartland has been dotted with extensive fields of agaves since the start of the seventeenth century.

During the nineteenth century, the uplands east of Guadalajara began to vie with the heartland for its share of the industry. Los Altos, "the highlands" as this Jaliscan region is called, is perched some six hundred to nine hundred meters higher than the *zona centro*, or "core zone" around Tequila. That core is where growers produced the slowly fermented tequilas known as Siete Liguas, Don Julio, Tres Magueyes, El Viejito, Don Felipe, and Centinela. The towns of Atotonilco el Alto, Tepatitlan de Morelos, and Arandas don't receive the traffic or notoriety that Tequila and Amatitán receive, but the distinctive quality of their products cannot be dismissed. Los Altos acreage now accounts for 46.4 percent of the tequila plantations in Jalisco; the zona centro around Tequila retains 51.6 percent of the acreage, and the lowland municipality of Tonaya in southern Jalisco accounts for 2 percent.

These regions' soils share many of the same characteristics

and are dominated by volcanically derived cambisols and luvisols (Valenzuela-Zapata 1992). If you pick up a clod of freshly plowed soil from any of these tequila-growing regions, you feel its clay siltiness between your fingers. It seldom has the rotting, fermenting smell of more organically rich soils, and it does not hold onto water as a peat or a muck soil would. Its colors range from coffee to ochre and rose, but the locals simply call them *colorados*. They are typically more than forty centimeters deep and nearly neutral in acidity (INEGI 1997). The cambisols have poorly developed profiles and tend to be richer in iron, silica, and aluminum. With time, as finer and finer particles accumulate and create a deeper, more developed lower profile, the cambisols evolve into what is known as luvisols (Fitzpatrick 1984).

Despite the myth that tequila comes from cactus-studded desert country, the tequila-growing regions are subhumid and subtropical rather than truly arid. Tropical prickly pears and candelabra-shaped columnar cacti do occur there, but an authentic desert plant would no doubt drown in the six hundred to twelve hundred millimeters of annual rainfall in tequila's heartland. Its hot, subhumid climate does not deter summer greenery; six hundred to eight hundred millimeters of rainfall can drop between June and October, transforming straw-colored pastures into a riot of verdure. Where the blue agave variety has been planted with less than six hundred millimeters of rainfall available to it, its growth is so slow and its harvests are so poor that the labor is hardly paid for by the product. When planted in areas with more than one thousand millimeters of rainfall, extremely well-drained soils are a necessity or else rotting sneaks in and diseases become more problematic. The more temperate areas of Los Altos typically produce a crop in eight to nine years instead of six to seven years.

The microclimates around Los Altos and the zona centro buffer mescal plants from leaf temperatures that would stress them beyond their physiological capacity to recover. In agronomic terms, the limiting factors for tequila agaves are temperatures below 3° to 10°C, or above 34°C. The photosynthetically optimal temperatures for tequila agave leaves are reached when ambient temperatures average about 15°C at night and 30°C during the day (Nobel and Valenzuela-Zapata 1987). Such temperature optima are frequently achieved in microclimates found in four agrohabitats in Jalisco: the barrancas, ranging from eight hundred to one thousand meters in elevation; the valleys and undulating plains closest to Tequila, ranging from one thousand to thirteen hundred meters in elevation; the intermediate zones of slopes and ridge tops, rising to thirteen hundred to seventeen hundred meters in elevation; and the mesa tops of Los Altos, which extend from seventeen hundred to twenty-one hundred meters in elevation. Although an elevation range of thirteen hundred meters poses different risks at either extreme, a tequila farmer can choose sunny slopes in Los Altos or bottomlands with cold air drainage in the zona centro to keep his plants in their comfort zone.

The Landscape Ecology of Agave-Culture in Tequila

The dominant agricultural landscape around the town of Tequila is agave monoculture, a genetically uniform crop planted in densities of twenty-five hundred to three thousand plants per hectare. Being in the center of origin of tequila production, the approximately 6,800 inhabitants of the municipality of Tequila now have few economic activities other than the cultivation, production, packaging, and sale of this alcoholic beverage. Roughly one-fourth (1,750) of all inhabitants of Tequila work in the fields, and at least another 1,200 work in distilling, bottling, packaging, or promoting tequila (INEGI 1997). Overall, 12,000 field hands are needed to keep the agricultural landscape of tequila production functioning as it does today, and these mescaleros form 5 percent of Jalisco's total agricultural workforce. The mescaleros, especially the jimadores, are the keepers of a legacy of traditional knowledge that maintains agave-culture in the agrohabitats we see today.

Although agaves are the only horticultural crop cultivated over much of this landscape, grazing is allowed in the plantations just prior to the harvest. While livestock compact the soil and trample younger plants, they also control weeds and manure the fields. Today, polycultures of agaves intercropped with maize, peanuts, or squashes can hardly be seen near Tequila, even though they were the prevailing forms of agriculture up until the "tequila boom." The only intercropping tradition to survive is the planting of maize between hedgerows of agaves that are less than two years old.

This blue-tinted agrohabitat is nested in a larger, greener landscape shaped by the Barranca de Tequila, an enormous volcanic canyon complex, and by the town's tutelary mountain, known to some as the "Cerro de Tequila." These landforms are set against the backdrop of a spur range of the formidable Sierra Madre Occidental. The entire landscape was set in place during the Tertiary period, with most of the ridges, canyon walls, and mesas formed by volcanic igneous intrusives (CENTENAL 1981).

As you rise out of the barrancas and into the valleys and plains where most plantations occur, you may find yourself putting on and taking off your sweater or jacket as you pass through various microclimates. And yet the prevailing climate is warm temperate, with temperatures oscillating between 22°C and 26°C for much of the year. The hotter months of May and June bring on drought stress severe enough for you to observe its effect on otherwise healthy plants. You can see how the leaves are not as fully extended, shifting their angles to reduce their exposure to damaging solar radiation. The leaves also pucker up as heat and drought stress set in, further reducing radiation damage and water loss by minimizing leaf area. On the other hand, on plants shaded much of the day by nearby trees, you can see more flaccid leaves; these mescal plants typically have larger but fewer leaves. Nearby in the barrancas, three other wild species of agaves exhibit similar heliotropic behavior. Leaf angles, surface areas, and reflectance values can shift as light intensities, cloudiness, or drought influence them. A rosette of agave leaves is not a static sphere, but an adaptable organism shaping its architecture to the climatic conditions prevailing during its lifetime.

Thanks to the antiquity of agave-culture around Tequila, its mescaleros are well-versed in reading the behavior of mescal plants, discerning their needs, and working to satisfy them. Much of this is done with traditional technologies that serve to help aerate the soil, improve infiltration, or reduce competition for moisture and nutrients. The mescaleros of Tequila shape their plantations with the use of two tools hardly used in other mescal-growing regions: the *coa de limpia* and the *machete barbeador.*

With these tools in hand, they are intent on controlling weeds, on trimming their plants whenever required, and in keeping the topsoil in good condition.

Nevertheless, as the external demand for tequila has intensified, mescaleros have painfully realized that their traditional knowledge and skills are not enough to ensure high yields from a genetically uniform monoculture increasingly vulnerable to plagues and diseases. The industry that purchases their agricultural product while demanding uniformity must now provide both technological support and technical knowledge for the mescaleros to produce the same yields per hectare that they achieved in previous decades. The monoculture of a genetically uniform crop has its downsides, especially when the entire local economy is dependent on it. Without a diversified economy, the jimador who is met with crop failure can hardly shift to another livelihood; more likely, he ends up in the cantina, drinking away his woes. The overproduction of tequila agaves, an after-effect of the "boom," favored the genetic uniformity that now makes the entire tradition of agave-culture more vulnerable than it has ever been before. Today, 96 percent of the mescaleros in the Tequila municipality have chosen to use herbicides or insecticides to maintain their crop yields, and 93 percent have chosen to use synthetic fertilizers instead of, or in conjunction with, organic manures (INEGI 1997).

Only 5 percent of the mescaleros of Tequila have found ways to break even without investing in modern agro-industrial chemicals and related technologies (INEGI 1997). Despite the perception that 100-percent-agave fructose-sugar tequilas are natural, "organic" products, their producers are as dependent upon the multinational agrochemical industry as any other farmers are elsewhere in the world. Monsanto, Dow, and Ceiba-Geigy now shape the production of tequila as much as the traditional knowledge of the wisest jimador does. Today's mescalero must know the ins-and-outs of using Captan, Metasystox, Cuprimic, and Formol as much as he knows the orally transmitted knowledge about *tocones, tostones, deshijes,* and *arrastres.* Roughly a fifth of all mescaleros in Tequila today rely on academically trained technical consultants, and roughly half of these are employed by agribusiness to promote the purchase of synthetic chemicals (INEGI 1997). Those who do not pay technical consultants still pick up much of their propaganda by word-of-mouth, billboards, or banter with supply store salesmen. It is fair to say that however fundamental the traditional knowledge of mescaleros is in maintaining agave-culture, it is being eclipsed by the necessity of dealing with pesticides, production contracts, and bank loans.

The Higher, Slower Zone: Los Altos

There is something different about Los Altos; it is truly higher ground. The activities of its rural inhabitants are more diversified than in Tequila. Every crop, from seasonal vegetables to the finest fruit trees, can be cultivated there with some success. But not everyone in the Jaliscan highlands makes their living as a farmhand; they also work in clothing factories, in cattle-raising, on hog farms, and in hatcheries. Agave-growing, as a business, has less stature and less history than around Tequila, but its presence can nevertheless be felt in every community.

Even though Los Altos now holds some 46 percent of all tequila-producing operations in Jalisco, they are less intensive, and more dispersed. The Jaliscan highlands are dotted with modest-sized villages, and more private landowners running small, diversified farms. In attempting to maximize the use of their heterogeneous landscape, they often intensively plant agaves on steep slopes where other crops or livestock won't be as productive. Their tequila plantings are often so dense that you can hardly walk through them.

The Los Altos region is characterized by a mosaic of volcanic ridges, mesas, plains, and mountains. The mescaleros who cultivate land on the limited number of mesa tops do best, but those whose work is relegated to the slopes are hardly slackers. They are all risk-takers, aggressively attempting to produce tequila close to its elevation limits, hoping to gain enough in the favorable seasons to tide them over during the years following catastrophic freezes. The frost and snow of December 1997 practically made margarita slurries out of all Los Altos mescal plantations, even before the tequila was extracted from them.

While most of the Los Altos soils are luvisols, which occur near Tequila as well, they are more frequently enriched by the organic manures of poultry, hogs, and cattle. They are also richer in iron, have higher clay content, and are slightly more acidic than those in the zona centro. The abundance of organic manures available in the region may reinforce the soil acidity, and sometimes they are too excessively applied to the highland soils. The highlanders are much more aggressive in their care for the soil, and have traditionally manured the other field crops, as well as the agave plantations. Amazingly, the highlanders pack five thousand plants into each hectare of agave production, nearly twice the average density in Tequila.

Such high densities require intensive care, particularly during the first three years after planting. As the stand reaches full cover, weeds are shaded out and the loss of soil moisture due to competition is greatly reduced. The highlanders usually achieve "total vegetative cover" of the soil by the time their agaves reach five years of age, but these densities then make them less prone to hoe or prune plantings close to maturity.

The highlanders are proud, hard-working conservatives, both religious and pragmatic in their outlook on life. Their social ties to one another have slowed the entry of agribusiness entrepreneurs into their homeland, so large-scale industrial agriculture has not gained much of a foothold in Los Altos. And yet, while a mescalero in Atotonilco el Alto is twice as likely to manure his mescal as is a mescalero in Tequila, he is just as likely to use a tractor, pesticides, or bank loans to get along (INEGI 1997). Nevertheless, each agricultural operation in Los Altos averages only three hectares in agave plantations, whereas the average operation in Tequila works ten hectares of agaves. The highlanders are no less prone to investing in modern agricultural technologies as their competitors in Tequila, but they have somehow resisted putting all of their arable lands into one mescal-flavored basket; they remain diverse.

How Does Agave-Culture Benefit Jalisco?

Because Jalisco has remained the world's leader in tequila production for well over a century and a half, it should be no surprise that agave-culture has shaped the economic and cultural landscape of the state in other ways. The production chain begun with the planting of an agave offshoot does not end with the first drop of alcohol siphoned into a bottle. The National Chamber of the Tequila Industry (CNIT) claims that it directly employs 23,202 local residents, including 20,000 field hands. Aside from mescaleros in the field, another 1,810 blue collar workers labor in the selection, sorting, mashing, fermentation, distillation, and bottling of tequila. Another 1,300 employees provide administrative support, and some 92 technical specialists provide professional (white collar) support for the industry. This workforce increased 14 percent in its number of employees between 1990 and 1994 (INEGI 1997). At least six new distillation plants opened over that time period.

Nevertheless, the overproduction of agaves in the zona tequilera should, sooner or later, have an impact on reducing the workforce. As the price of tequila drops, as is expected, greater unemployment and out-migration are likely to follow. With fewer jobs available for the most experienced jimadores, employers will have an easier time filling any job without paying a premium salary to those with the greatest grasp of traditional skills.

The thirty-six hundred agave-producing farm operations in Jalisco attend to the demands of nearly fifty distillation plants, but these producers remain fragmented in their negotiations with buyers. The structure of supply and demand cycles now favor the buyers of tequila agaves, since cultivators of a perennial crop have less flexibility in adjusting their production to short-term shifts in demand. Until the tequila industry fully exploits other optional markets, such as those of the high-fructose sugars now found in the Anheuser-Busch beer named "Tequiza," producers will remain at the mercy of nearly fifty tequila distilleries. Ironically, there is already a backlash from the sugar cane industry against the tequila producers' attempts to diversify their buyers. Sugar industry consultants have released scathing (but largely unfounded) indictments of the health risks potentially resulting from the "unhygienic" production and extraction of agave sugars, and even assert that all high-fructose sugars may pose health risks. Until tequila farmers counter this negative publicity and secure long-term contracts with the producers of specialty foods and drinks, they will have little power in their negotiations with the distilleries.

As far as competition among tequila farmers goes, the highlanders have the edge. Buyers prefer the high-sugar, high-moisture, and low-fiber content of their raw materials, produced under a climate that is less stressful except for occasional frosts. The zona centro can hardly achieve these same qualities, except from select plants taken from the choicest sites. Climate, plant management, traditions, and economic histories have shaped what each region offers in volume, flavor, and labeling. The workaday rhythms and size of Los Altos and the zona centro also differ. The same blue agave, cultivated by these two mescalero traditions, takes on a different identity and context in each landscape, creating a rivalry that many savor.

Dreaming the Future of Tequila

ι ι ι

"[The boom] began in Europe, when the high society of Paris discovered this drink that was so maltreated all over the world, and realized that in addition to it being an exquisite beverage, it had an impressive history with roots tracing back before the Conquest. And so, tequila began to captivate the European palate, which was when Mexicans going to Europe discovered that their national drink was famous there, and returning to Mexico, they began to drink it and promote it in their social circles. But the other factor in this boom, above all else in Mexico, was that women were now considered the strongest market for tequila. What we don't know is why they have so much fondness for this drink."
—Antonio Garcia, liquor store owner

The National Drink of Exiled Songsters and Novelists

What will the future offer tequila and other mescals? Tequila and its kin, at least in the eyes and mouths of U.S. citizens, has changed its image from a generic liquor or "firewater" to a drink of the elite. It now also has an undeniable place in pop culture. You can find tequila in song and in film as frequently as you can find it in the bars and lounges of the hipsters and yuppies. Today, this Mexican beverage has gained respect not only in the border states of the Southwest, but in all parts of the United States. Its dubious reputation as a near-hallucinogen has grown large, inflated by the mescal-flavored writings of Malcolm Lowry, Charles Bowden, and Hunter S. Thompson. It has also soared in the songs of Hoyt Axton, Tom Russell, Robert Earl Keen, Jim Reeves, and Jimmy

Buffett, just as it had decades before in the *corridos* and *sones* of Los Alegres de Teran and Antonio Aguilar.

From Cowboys to Coeds

Whoever has asked "Why did the tequila boom happen?" has no doubt wondered about the way tequila serves as a barometer of social climate. Once, only cowboys drank cheap tequila in border towns; then, jocks and coeds discovered margaritas on their way down to Mexican beaches for spring vacations; today, new age entrepreneurs in Boulder and Burlington sip ultra-premium aged tequilas alongside other fashionable spirits in fancy bars, lodges, and bed-and-breakfasts.

And yet, we remember, like a flashback from an old charro film, the image of the poor drunk holding a bottle of tequila in one hand, and gesturing for his lost love with the other, singing his sad refrain about "mas copitas de mescal." Can this be the same beverage drunk by well-educated youth discussing Latin American ecotourism and cultural history in exclusive restaurants? Does it fuel the same desires? Is Two Fingers Tequila, regardless of its makeover, still (merely) mescal?

Paradigm Shifting from Firewater to the Seasoned Essence of Mescal

Mexico has once again embraced its tequilas, just as these mescals have become a symbol of international status. When you now give a Mexican friend an aged bottle of tequila, it is a prestigious present, reaffirming his identity. At the same time, cheap tequilas are spoken of more pejoratively than ever before, for they have become synonymous with adulteration and terrible hangovers. Mexican connoisseurs tend to prefer the white and reposado tequilas, whereas their neighbors to the north buy more "gold." This is ironic, since the only known mescal bacanora bottled in the United States was promoted at the turn of the century by Tucson's Julius Goldbaum as "crystalline white," to differentiate it from rotgut *sotol* and mescal from farther south. In both the country of origin and the most popular destination point, it is no longer the fad to chug a shot of cheap-tasting tequila, then chase away the roughness in your throat by sucking on a lime. Today, the favored tequilas are smooth, almost silky, like sipping whiskeys, so that even the most timid of young ladies no longer fear to sample them.

In the United States today, premium tequila captures a respectable niche in the market of distillates destined for thirty to fifty year olds. These "older" consumers compare their favorite tequilas to brandies, bourbons, and scotches. However, other brands of tequila are packaged and promoted to lure twenty to thirty-five year olds away from party-time beer and wines. Yet another tequila market strategy is aimed at those who wish to show to their friends that they are always in hot pursuit of some thing new and different, worth its cost because it represents the finest quality available. Curiously, these high-end consumers avoid the tequila labels that are gaudy, as well as rich colors in the tequilas themselves, the latter appearing too much like herbal remedies. They may not drink as much as the regulars at the local cantina's happy hour, but they pay more to sip than their rowdy friends pay to down tequila shooters.

The Mix-up about Mescal, Mescal Bean, and Mescalito

Despite two decades of "tequila fever" in the United States, many of its disciples still confuse it with "cactus juice," or claim that it contains residual mescaline that makes them psychotropically "high" rather than functioning as a depressant, as all alcohol does. The mescalito extracted from the peyote cactus *(Lophophora williamsii)*, the mescal bean *(Sophora segundiflora)*, and the mescal for the mescal plant *(Agave* species) are not botanically related or chemically analogous. All three occurred within the former range of the Mescalero Apache and mescaline-dropping hippies, but there the affinity ends.

Cantinas as Proving Grounds

Without a doubt, the second tequila boom was propelled by the popularity of Tex-Mex restaurants, first in the desert borderlands, then in other regions of the United States as well. These restaurants gradually shifted from sharing a single tequila with their clientele, to offering one white and one gold, to the current rage of featuring a half dozen sipping tequilas, each on a different night. To stay ahead of their more studious customers, waiters have learned to be well-versed in the qualities of each brand name, as well as the nuances of aging or *"añejamiento."*

The rapid refinement of taste and shifting appreciation of tequila's history have led to old drinking habits dying as new rituals emerge. It is now generally considered a waste for a bartender or waitress to serve a margarita made with an aged or rested tequila; special (usually cheaper) stock is used exclusively for this chore. Mescal connoisseurs have developed a sophisticated understanding of the salutary effects of various aging processes, echoing the traditional mescalero's more rustic terms and gestures for describing bottles that are finely seasoned, fully mature, or mildly effervescent.

Another recent revelation for foreign consumers of tequila—but one that Jaliscans have understood for decades—is that tequilas distilled 100 percent from agave sugars have qualities undeniably distinct from those of tequilas cut with cane sugars. This particularity is now underscored on the labels of premium tequilas, and has become the most direct assurance of authenticity and quality.

That said, what might happen next to tequilas and other mescals? Will producers opt to promote further recognition of tequila's many faces and tastes? Over the years, the legal definition and market niche of tequila has gradually changed. Mexico's Official Norms for tequila today are much more precisely defined than they were decades ago, so that current specifications clearly favor the largest, most industrialized producers. It is important to stress that today, many decisions are in the hands of the government's regulating council, CRIT; whereas in the past, the producers themselves were the final judges of their own products. Despite this squeeze toward uniformity, the foreign consumer delights in a diversity of flavors and fragrances, and has to date kept tequila's progress from being anything but dull. Because the United States remains the most lucrative market for tequileros to capture, the changing habits and perceptions of American drinkers are the code to decipher. Whether Mexicans like it or not, the destiny of tequila is shaped more and more by the imaginations of its American consumers, who are savoring a complex of rich cultural and emotive associations as much as they are imbibing an alcoholic beverage.

We are reminded of Malcolm Lowry's (1971) tequila-drinking tragedy, *Under the Volcano:*

> But without mescal, he imagined, he had forgotten eternity, forgotten their world's voyage, that the earth was a ship, lashed by the Horn's tail, doomed. . . . [And then] suddenly he saw them . . . the beautiful bottles of tequila, the gourds, gourds, gourds, the millions of gourds of beautiful mescal. . . . The Consul sat very still. His conscience sounded muffled with the roar of water. . . . How indeed could he hope to find himself, to begin again. When, somewhere, perhaps, in one of those lost or broken bottles, in one of those glasses, lay, forever, the solitary clue to his identity?

Sipping and Internet Surfing: Future Strategies for Fostering Tequila

Tequila taste tests in the United States indicate that most drinkers now shun any brands with a rough or bitter aftertaste, favoring those that have a more delicate herbal flavor that does not overwhelm the "essence of agave." The Americans interviewed who express the most pleasure in drinking tequilas claim that it is the individuality of each 100-percent-agave tequila that they like, for each of these premium tequilas has its own peculiar traits. These fine tequilas now comprise only 1 percent of the total production, but they will increasingly influence the destiny of the entire agro-industry.

Consumers are no longer satisfied with having the taste of tequilas buried beneath ice, lemon, salt, and grenadine. They are subtly intrigued by the flavors of volcanic earth, oak barrel, and herb that mix in ways that tease their noses, tongues, lips, eyes, and throats. Home pages on the Internet devoted to tequila have begun to share empirical tests and professional opinions of various brands. Some of the "tequilleurs" quoted on these home pages speak of savoring the "perfect" tequila as a sacred experience.

However obvious it is to Jaliscan producers of tequila, most consumers have yet to pay much attention to the sensual or organoleptic differences between the distillates from Los Altos and those from the zona centro. They seldom even notice the differences in flavor between true Jaliscan tequilas and those from the states of Tamaulipas or Guanajato, where both climate and soils are unlike those of either Tequila and Los Altos. Without any doubt, the nuances of regional variation in tequila maturation and distillation traditions will garner increasing interest from those who give special attention to 100-percent-agave tequilas. Locally, certain Jaliscans already listen for the echoes of landscape and climate reverberating in each tequila bottle, but consumers elsewhere have not yet opened their ears to such music.

Pricing Tequilas: Balancing Expense with Value

Tequila producers have only recently become aware of what consumers are saying about their brands over the Internet and through "chat room" list servers linked by e-mail. Regardless of whether such commentaries offered over e-mail are representative of larger constituencies of consumers, some anecdotes are now being dispersed with lightning speed all around the world. For instance, electronic folk historians of tequila claim that it was a European who first positioned 100-percent-agave premium tequilas on the high end of distilled beverages. Without even being an owner or a manager of a tequila distillery, this promoter designed a marketing strategy that has raised some tequila brands to mythic status by using elegant bottles and labels that are rich in folk cultural connotations. He began to import tequila to Europe, the United States, and Canada, where he found consumers willing to pay prices so high that they were at the time unimaginable to Mexico's distilleries. Since then, many others have followed this strategy of marketing not just the beverage itself, but an entire set of designs, names, slogans, and derivative products that collectively capture a market previously unanticipated by Jaliscan entrepreneurs. This strategy has not yet been as successful in Mexico, where producers remain careful not to price their tequilas higher than the average consumer can pay.

There are other factors constraining another meteoric rise or "boom" for 100-percent-agave tequilas. Tequilas and other mescals are among the few distilled spirits produced anywhere in the world that are made from plants with long life cycles, and that also require long periods to ferment, distill, and age. As the current epidemic demonstrates, other unforeseen factors can suddenly reduce the supply of agaves to the industry, so that reserves are slowly depleted over several years' time. These factors work in concert to slow the tequila industry's response time to market trends and fads.

Fortunately, the industry's own trajectory is now placing a premium on tequilas elaborated from 100-percent-agave sugars, then slowly and carefully aged in oak barrels. The benefit of this care is that shots of premium tequilas demand twenty-five to fifty dollars in California cantinas, and ultra-super premiums sell for two thousand dollars even when they are not accompanied by a handblown, artisan-designed bottle.

Who Would Have Thunk It?

A half century ago, who would have believed that tequila sales would increase 15 percent annually for most of the last three decades, or that the prices of premium tequilas would ever eclipse those of champagnes? While tequila still occupies less than 4 percent of the sales of distilled alcoholic beverages around the world, its growth rate has recently surpassed all others, with a quarter million more cases of tequila consumed one year than the year before.

The second tequila boom in the United States is even more enigmatic. While the U.S. consumption of distilled alcohol has recently dropped by 22 percent, the sales of tequila to U.S. consumers increased 31 percent over the same period of time. Liquor stores have witnessed a 40 percent rise in tequila sales over the last two years. The number of tequila brands marketed in the United States has doubled in just five years' time. And, as already hinted, tequilas produced from 100-percent-agave sugars have witnessed a 62.4 percent increase in sales, while other tequilas garnered only a 15.6 percent increase in sales. Whereas tequila imports to the United States collectively rose 16.5 percent from 1995 to 1996, most of the added value of these sales came from premium tequilas (INEGI 1997).

What Changes Are Bound to Come?

American consumers believe that tequila producers are greatly improving the quality of products by better controlling the distillation and aging processes. This is a brilliant marketing strategy, for it has signaled connoisseurs that the industry is responsive to their tastes. The "new tequilas" produced with greater quality control command higher prices, of course, if only for their elaborate bottle and label designs, which reassure consumers that they are savoring a distillate of unprecedented smoothness and purity.

American consumers have readily greeted every new innovation with appreciation. With a wider range of tequilas available, aficionados are happier than ever. Some restaurants now give awards to regular customers who have distinguished themselves as tequila connoisseurs. The labeling of premium tequilas now allows information to be disseminated along with the beverage in a way that promotes social parlance among devotees regarding each tequila's distinctive qualities. But now that there is a groundswell of American folk opinion associated with various tequilas, how does this change the marketing strategies of the various distilleries? Should their propaganda attempt to follow popular opinion, or should it divert American attention to other choices? Just a few brands of tequila are wildly popular in the United States among devotees, while others that are equally excellent in quality have not yet entered the limelight. American bars and restaurants no longer doubt that their clients desire to be educated about a wider range of tequilas, but their buyers remain influenced by salesmen's pitches, contract obligations, and other constraints. The education that bars offer their customers, in other words, is powerfully shaped by economic considerations.

Without doubt, liquor salesmen have had great success in pushing tequilas as indispensable components of Mexican-American cuisine, realizing that spicy foods have developed into the fastest growing culinary industry in the United States over the last two decades. These salesmen realize the significance of salsa recently eclipsing catchup as America's most frequently consumed condiment. A great diversity of chile peppers and salsas have flooded the American marketplace, displacing older, blander hot sauce brands just as the new tequilas have narrowed the niche occupied by Jose Cuervo Gold. Tequilas are now promoted along with Southwestern, Mexican-American, Texican, and Latino foods in culinary magazines, on television, on the radio, and on the Internet. While tequila's most sophisticated devotees lament the abundance of misinformation promulgated by these ad campaigns, at least they can confidently go into any Mexican restaurant today and find several brands of tequila.

The outcome of all this promotion still may come as a surprise to most Anglo-Americans. Tequilas have now displaced whiskeys as the most frequently consumed spirit in the United States. The bourbons and scotches of the Anglo-Saxon tradition have taken a backseat to the peculiarly New World tequilas, grandchildren of the pre-Hispanic mescal. Tequila is now treated more like cognac or grappa, and no longer grouped with Thunderbird, Tokay, and Everclear as a cheap, quick means to become *muy borracho*.

Will Other Mescals Ride in on Tequila's Coattails?

We hope that other mescals will soon follow the same wondrous trajectories that well-made tequilas have. Sotol, bacanora, la raicilla, and mescal de Oaxaca are being revived to respectability and establishing their own quality standards; the diversity of tastes available to connoisseurs of mescal is broadening. If such competition is good for business, perhaps it will also allow tequila growers to broaden their crops' genetic base once again, reacquainting themselves with the wild and primitive ancestors of blue agave. Already their customers have shown a willingness to taste unblended batches of ancestral mescal, cared for with all the sophistication that the last century and a half of growth have brought to the industry.

Bring on the Flowers, Bring in the Pollinators

If the botanical rediversification of the tequila industry is indeed possible, perhaps growers will be prosperous enough to let a few rows of mescal flower every now and then, helping to feed the bats that still migrate northward through their region on the nectar trail each spring. We are currently working with the Proyecto para la Conservación de Murcielagos Migratorios and the Partners in Pollination Alliance to evaluate whether flowering agaves in the zona centro can benefit endangered nectar-feeding bats and rediversify the blue agave gene pool. While the final word is not yet in, we predict that reestablishing the ancient connection between bats and agaves will benefit everyone involved. Our hope is that tequila drinkers everywhere will support such experiments, realizing that tequila tastes even better when you can be assured that your beverage is benefiting both local communities and native wildlife.

Appendix 1

A Mescalero's Lexicon

⚊ ⚊ ⚊

The following vocabulary of "folk technical terms" includes words used by mescaleros throughout Mexico in their daily work with agaves, from plant selection through harvesting and distillation. If a term is used solely, or in a unique way, in a specific region, a locational marker will follow the term in parentheses. If used throughout the tequila-producing areas, the term is not followed by any location marker in parentheses. Terms are derived from our own field notes, and from Valenzuela-Zapata (1997); Sobarzo (1991); Cabrera (1994); García-Mendoza (1998); Bye, Burgess, and Tryan (1975); Bahre and Bradbury (1980); Parsons and Parsons (1990); and other sources.

Achicalar. To "harden" or "rest" recently excavated and separated vegetative offshoots, so that prior to their transplanting, they can scar over blade cuts made to the leaves and rhizomes. This period of hardening seldom lasts more than ten days.

Acordonar. The heaping together of cut, dried weeds to burn. These weeds are cleaned from between the rows in the agave plantation, and then taken to the edge of the field to burn.

Acuartelar. The action of delimiting a field plantation of agaves from adjacent plantings, done by contouring the soil with tractors and plows.

Almagre. Clayey soil of low fertility that results in low-productivity agave plantations.

Amacizar (Valle de México). Regional synonym of "achicalar" (see above).

Arranque. The removal of vegetative offshoots from the mother plant by cutting the connective rhizome with tools such as the *barretón* and *azadón*, the latter of which often injures the offshoot.

Arrastre. The final harvest in the last year of a plantation, including the removal of all plants, regardless of their maturity and quality.

Aseda. This term is used when vegetative offshoots die as a result of poor ventilation in their holding-grounds, or in the process of disinfection or transport.

Bacanora/mescal bacanora. A bootleg mescal made from the northernmost populations of *Agave angustifolia* var. *pacifica* in Sonora and adjacent Chihuahua, sometimes mixed with *lechuguilla* from *A. palmeri,* where the two
species co-occur. Named for the small rancheria of Bacanora near the
pueblo of Sahuaripa, Sonora, this mescal was recently legalized and com-
mercialized, but the clandestine cottage industry product by this name
remains the pride of Sonorans.

Barbeo. This is the generic term for any pruning or trimming of agave leaves,
but it also refers specifically to the action of cutting the spines and leaf tips
off upper leaves. The mescaleros of Los Altos do not frequently attempt as
many variants of pruning and trimming as the Tequila area mescaleros do,
who adapt the trimming process to the age, size, and health status of the
plants.

Barbeo de arbolito/farol. This preventive trimming is done even when leaf pests,
diseases, or abiotic stress have not yet become apparent. It is typically done
to plantations four years old or older as a means to promote better aera-
tion and solar gain.

Barbeo de cacheteo (Tequila) or *chaponeo* (Los Altos). Referring to pruning to
gain access between agave rows in the plantation, this effort involves trimming the basal and median leaves that overlap those of adjacent rows.

Barbeo de desemplague. This selective trimming is applied to remove the larvae
known as *gusano barrenador,* by targeting leaves that show early signs of
damage.

Barbeo de escobeta, banco rebajado, or *castigado.* This is the most intensive pruning, in which the length of all leaves, including the terminal bud, is cut in
half, creating a flat-topped form. Researchers have shown that this treatment permits greater solar gain so that the trimmed plants complete their
maturation process much more rapidly. However, this accelerated maturation technique cannot be used on plants under five years of age.

Barbeo de semilla. Referring to the pruning done to prepare plants for the
arranque extraction of offshoots, this process results in trimmed basal leaves
and terminal spines on adjacent leaves.

Barranco (Sonora-Chihuahua). The stone-lined earthen oven, often sealed with
clay, where agaves are pit-roasted.

Barrial. This term is used to refer to lands with modest sloping but considerable clay content that are prone to erosion, leaving only clay without any
organic matter.

Biguata (Sonora-Chihuahua). The "heart" or meristem of an agave, sometimes
roasted and then added to distilled mescal to flavor it.

Bola. This pruned-back agave rosette contains both the meristem and the leaf
bases of the plant, so that it looks like a pineapple, ball, or head.

Caballo/cabezas. The first run of mescal through the still, sometimes called
"mescal ordinario" or "tequila ordinario."

Cabeza. Same as "bola" (see above).

Cacheteo. See "barbeo de cacheteo" (above).

Calavarea. It is said that a plantlet is a calavarea when it won't "take" and grow after being transplanted. The term is also used when the offshoot's rhizomes were pruned too short during their removal from the mother plant.

Calle. Same as "loma" (see below).

Callejón. The "aisles" or interspaces within and on the edges of an agave plantation, which permit the movement of mescaleros during their fieldwork.

Capada. The "castration" or removal of an agave's emerging inflorescence scape to thicken or enrich the vegetative tissues with sugars.

Capona. Same as "capada" (see above).

Careo (Valle de México). The removal of newly emerged inflorescence scapes to obtain aguamiel and to process pulque.

Cazanga. See "cazangueo" (below).

Cazangueo. The cleaning or weeding of the plantation's interspaces, done with a hooked tool called a "cazanga." It is sometimes done just before herbicide applications to cut back weeds so that their leaves don't overlap with those of the agaves, as a means to reduce herbicide application to the agaves themselves.

Ceboruco. Volcanic soils that contain so much basaltic cobbles and boulders that farm machinery cannot be used on them. Although the term is used in the Tequila area, it originally referred to soils surrounding Volcán Ceboruco in the nearby state of Nayarit.

Chaponeo (Los Altos and Tequila). This term has different meanings in Los Altos and Tequila. When used in the Jaliscan highlands, it refers to the pruning or cutting of leaves to allow access to the interspaces between rows, a process called "cacheteo" in Tequila. In the lower country, "chaponeo" refers specifically to the cleaning done with a cazanga.

Chautoso. This clayey soil has poor drainage and is often left with standing water after rains, which aggravates plant diseases in agaves.

Chicata (Sonora-Chihuahua). The meristem or base of the terminal bud that forms the heart of an agave.

Chicote (Sonora-Chihuahua). Same as "tumbayaquis" (see below).

Chirrión. This is the folk term used to describe the rhizomes connecting mother plants with their vegetative offshoots; it is not a true root but a modified stem.

Churri (Sonora-Chihuahua). Deflowered or "castrated" agaves that become more massive and sugar-rich. By removing the emerging flower stalk and breaking apical dominance several months before harvesting, traditional Sonoran mescaleros promote vegetative offshooting to regenerate the clonal population, and concentrate the plant's sugars in the meristem and leaf bases rather than losing them to sexual reproductive effort. This traditional wild agave management technique may have begun among Opata Indians, but is being lost among newly arrived residents to Sonora, who deplete agave populations by not managing them in this manner.

Cirial (Oaxaca). A local name given to cultivars of *Agave karwinskii* used in making *mescal de la olla*.

Cogollo. The apical meristem and its terminal bud. If this is damaged just prior to flowering, either by cutting (capona) or by herbicides such as 2,4,5-D, apical dominance is broken and lateral branches (offshoots connected by rhizomes and leaf axils) may produce miniature flower stalks.

Cuguri (Sonora-Chihuahua). A local Sonoran *serrano* or Opata/Eudeve term for *cogollo* (see above).

Cuvino (Sonora-Chihuahua). A Yoeme (Yaqui Indian) term for distilled mescal, from *cuu* (*agave* in Yoeme) and *vino* (*wine* in Spanish). This term has been assimilated into Sonoran Spanish, but is not now used frequently outside of the Rio Yaqui watershed.

Desbote. This term refers to the deleafing or removal of offshoots that tax the development and thickening of the mother plant.

Descarne. When the labor of hoeing or tilling the soil is done poorly so that the roots of the agaves are exposed then left uncovered, desiccating them or slowing their growth.

Descorone. Same as "calavarea" (see above).

Desempiedre. The labor of removing cobbles from the volcanically derived soils in tequila fields.

Desemplaque. See "barbeo de desemplague" (above).

Deshije/desahij. Same as "arranque" (see above).

Desmonte. Same as "desvare" (see below); also used as a term for the elimination of natural vegetative cover to initiate the planting of agaves.

Desquiote. The action of removing the *quiote* or flower stalk in order to prevent flowering and subsequent plant desiccation; instead, apical dominance is broken, offshooting may be promoted, and the mother plant swells full of the sugars that would have otherwise fueled the rapid growth of the flower stalk.

Destronconar. The fieldwork needed to remove the remaining taproots and bases of plants left by incomplete harvesting by jimadores. The roots and "trunk" are unearthed and taken away in order to make the field ready for another planting.

Desvare. The labor required to eliminate herbaceous annual and perennial saplings *(varas)* so that agaves may be planted.

Dientes. The serrate lateral edges of an agave leaf.

Entresaque. The partial harvest of an agave plantation in the first year that any plants reach maturity.

Espadín. A folk taxon or varietal name used for a cultivated variety of *Agave angustifolia* in Oaxaca, as well as in parts of Jalisco.

Espinas. Same as "dientes" (see above).

Farol. See "barbeo de farol" (above).

Guardarraya. The controlled burn or the between-row plowing of weeds in the aisles (callejónes) of a plantation.

Hijuelo. The vegetative offshoot or "pup" found beneath the skirts of a mother plant, sometimes called "the seed." See "semilla" (below).

Hincado. A nickname for heavy plants near maturity that have partially fallen over.

Horno (Sonora-Chihuahua). Same as "barranco" (see above).

Huerta (Los Altos). The name given in the highlands to agave fields.

Jaivica (Sonora-Chihuahua). The axelike tool used in the jima, or harvest of mature agaves.

Jima. The harvest of agaves in which both leaves are trimmed and the mother plant is dislodged from its roots, done in Tequila with a hoe or pick that has a sharply filed circular blade.

Jima alta. The trimming for harvest in which no leaf bases extend past the spherical form of the agave head or "pineapple."

Jimador. The harvester who uses a sharpened blade, pry bar and/or axelike tool (see "jaivica" above) to accomplish the final trimming and uprooting of a mature agave. "El Jimador" is also the name of a popular brand of tequila.

Jima rasurada. This term is used for the well-executed trimming of agaves, which does not leave residual parts of the plants sticking out.

Lechuguilla (Jaliscan coastal lowlands and Sonora-Chihuahua). Although this term is most widely used for an agave from the Chihuahuan Desert that is only marginally suitable for mescal-making, it is also used for other, less sapogenin-laden species elsewhere. In the municipality of Mascota, Jalisco, mescal raicilla is made from lechuguilla *(Agave inaequidens)* and from "pata de ula" cultivars; it remains commercially available. In Sonora, Chihuahua, and southern Arizona, *A. palmeri* (including *A. shrevei*) were used both prehistorically and historically for food and drink. This species continues to be utilized by eastern Sonorans in the zona serrana to produce a distilled mescal also called "lechuguilla," but it is more typically mixed with *A. angustifolia* and distilled to make mescal bacanora.

Limpia. The removal of weeds from around maturing plants, done in Tequila and Los Altos with a specially forged tool called the "coa de limpia," which is used to remove any weeds within a meter's radius of the plant base.

Loma. The interspace between plants within the same row or furrow.

Maguey. Any large-sized agave species, but particularly those used for pulque production. This term was first encountered by Europeans in the islands of the Caribbean, and most likely has a Carib rather than Nahuatl origin. Nevertheless, it is curious that it is much like a contraction of the Nahuatl terms "metl" or "maitl," (agave) and *"huey"* (grand).

Maguey ancho (Guerrero). The folk name applied to *Agave cupreata*, a wild agave in the Rio Balsas of Guerrero and Michoacán, used for making distilled mescal. Langlasse, who first collected a specimen of this agave in 1899, noted that it was called "maguey de mescal" and was used to distill an alcohol also called "mescal."

Maguey espadín. Same as "espadín" (see above).

Margayate (Sonora-Chihuahua). A nearly forgotten term for bitter, poorly made bootleg mescal.

Mechichicual. The sawlike teeth on the edge of an agave leaf.

Mecuatl (Hidalgo). Vegetative offshoot emerging from the base of the mother plant through a rhizomatous connection.

Mescal/mezcal. Agave plants of species or cultivated varietal selections that serve in making the food, fermented beverage, or spirits that are referred to by this same name. Probably derived from the Nahuatl terms "metl" (agave) and *"ixcalli"* (roasted or baked).

Mescal bronco (Sonora-Chihuahua). The high-proof distillate obtained from the second run of a still, which is later mixed with the more watery first run.

Mescal casero (Sonora-Chihuahua). A cultivated variant of mescal bacanora or *gusime* cultivated in the Sierra Madre by the Western Tarahumara and their mestizo neighbors.

Mescal de cabeza/agua vina (Sonora-Chihuahua). The more watery first run of a mescal still, later mixed with "mescal bronco" (see above).

Mescalón (Sonora-Chihuahua). Same as "tumbayaquis" (see below).

Meyolote (Hidalgo). Terminal growth bud, or central leaf cluster.

Mezonte/mezontle. The meristem tissue of granular texture in the base or stem of the agave, that has the textural appearance of a mane. From the Nahuatl terms "metl" (agave) and *"tzontli,"* (mane).

Mochomos (Sonora-Chihuahua). Literally, this term refers to nocturnal leaf-cutter ants *(Atta mexicana).* Metaphorically, the term refers to night-working bootleggers of mescal bacanora and lechuguilla.

Palenque (Oaxaca). A distillery or winery where mescal is fermented and distilled.

Papolometl/papolomete. A diminutive agave cultivar of *Agave potatorum,* used in Oaxaca to produce mescal de la olla. The name is a Nahuatl contraction of *"papálotl"* (butterfly) and "metl" (agave).

Parcela. Same as "portero" (see below).

Penca. The succulent leaf of an agave (also a prickly pear pad or cladode).

Pica. The manual labor done with an azadón hoe to toss soil over potentially exposed roots and to incorporate cut, dried weeds into the soil as compost. In heavily sloping plantations, this fieldwork, if poorly done, can aggravate soil erosion.

Picado (Oaxaca). The cutting of agave heads for baking.

Piña. Same as "bola" (see above).

Potrero. In the Tequila region, these terms are used to refer to the parcels of land managed as agave plantations.

Quema. Same as "guardarraya" (see above).

Quiote. Flower stalk, technically, the scape of the inflorescence, sometimes roasted and eaten.

Razas criollas. These "folk varieties" or culturally selected clonal variants are all domesticated forms within the *Agave angustifolia* complex, treated here as cultivated varieties in subspecies *tequilana:* (1) Azul/blue agave: the most widely planted clonal variety of tequila, and the only one officially accepted by the Norma Oficial Mexicana; (2) Xigüin/sigüín: similar in traits to azul, it has narrower leaf bases and a greenish rather than bluish cast; (3) Bermejo: larger than azul, with longer, wider leaves that are slower growing; (4) Chato:

its thicker, greenish leaves have larger, broader spines; (5) Moraleño: smaller than azul, this variety has a lighter color, shorter leaves, and many more leaves per rosette.

Redrojo. A vegetative offshoot of poor quality, with undesirable characteristics, which is thrown away instead of being transplanted.

Saite (Sonora-Chihuahua). This term refers to juicy, sugar-rich fibrous material or chopped, fermented leaf bases of pit-roasted mescal; the discarded fiber and its residual sugars are then used as cattle fodder or as bagasse to be mixed into mud to strengthen adobe bricks.

Semilla. Mescaleros call the vegetative offshoots "seeds" or "disseminules" because they use them to establish new plantings; however, unlike most true seeds, the clonal offshoot is genetically identical to its mother plant.

Shishi (Oaxaca). "Ordinary mescal" after the first pass through the still.

Sierra. Same as "dientes" (see above).

Sorrascado. This name is given to agave plants with bases dried and shrunken by contact with fires or diseases.

Sotol (Sonora-Chihuahua). A distilled beverage made in the Chihuahuan Desert, and formerly, in Sonora, from the roasted, fermented heads of the desert spoon plant, *Dasylirion wheeleri*, using much the same methods as those used in making mescal. The state of Chihuahua now promotes commercial sotols.

Tocón. This term is used for the rhizomes of vegetative offshoots that are cut off their mother plants during the tostoneo. They are called "tocones" if, ideally, the circumference of the rhizome equals the now-obsolete tocón, a Mexican coin for 50 centavos, roughly two centimeters in diameter.

Trazo. The plantation design, defined by the direction and contour of the rows in which the agaves are planted, and laid out by string, rope, measuring tape, or tractor furrow.

Tren (Sonora-Chihuahua). A copper-coiled still, including a kettle and drumlike cap that form the distillation chamber.

Troncón. The base or stem of a maturing agave.

Tumbayaquis (Sonora-Chihuahua). High-proof mescal, strong enough to make a "stoic Yaqui warrior" fall.

Yunta. Same as "portrero" (see above).

Xinatli. Yeast or other fermenting agents.

Appendix 2

Common Names for Mescal-Producing Agaves in Spanish Dialects and Indigenous Languages Spoken in "Mega-Mexico"

▲ ▲ ▲

Agave americana L.: chato, maguey chichimeco, maguey meco, sahuayo, teometl

Agave angustifolia Haw. (including *A. tequilana* Weber): bacanora, bermejo, blue agave, chato, chino, chino azul, chino bermejo, criollo, espadín, maguey tequilero, mano de mula, mano larga, mescal azul, mescal bacanora, pata de mula, pie de mula, zapupe

Agave asperrima Jacobi: maguey del cerro

Agave capensis Gentry: mezcalito

Agave karwinskii Zucc.: cirial

Agave murpheyi F. Gibson: a'ud nonhakam

Agave palmeri Engelm. (including *A. shrevei* Gentry): lechuguilla, a'ud, totosá, totosali

Agave pelona Gentry: mescal pelón

Agave potatorum Zucc.: papalometl

Agave weberi Cels. ex Poisson: al-milamal

Agave wocomahi Gentry: uocomahi

Agave zebra Gentry: mescal lechuguilla

Appendix 3

Agave Species Domesticated Prehistorically for Food, Fiber, Hedge, or Beverage Uses by Indigenous Communities

❧ ❧ ❧

Agave americana L.: food, fiber, beverage, hedge
Agave angustifolia Haw.: food, fiber, beverage, hedge
Agave atrovirens Karw. ex Salm-Dyck.: beverage, hedge
Agave delamateri Hodgson & Slauson: food, fiber
Agave ferox Koch: see *A. salmiana*
Agave fourcroydes Lem.: fiber, hedge
Agave karwinskii Zucc.: hedge, beverage
Agave mapisaga Trel.: beverage, hedge
Agave murpheyi F. Gibson: food, fiber
Agave salmiana Otto ex. Salm.: beverage
Agave sisalana Perrine: fiber, hedge
Agave tequilana Weber: see *A. angustifolia*
Agave utahensis Engelm: food, fiber

Appendix 4

Species Description of Cultivated Agave Species
Historically Used in the Tequila Industry

⚜ ⚜ ⚜

Beginning in 1985, one of us (Ana) began to search for the various agaves that were historically used to produce tequila by mescaleros in western Mexico. This search was based on the descriptions of cultivated agaves made by Lázaro Pérez in 1887: azul, sigüín, moraleño, bermejo, chato, pie de mula, zopilote, mano larga, and mezcal chino. Only azul is still commonly cultivated. Over the years, we have continued to track down the other cultivars. With difficulty, we relocated the cultivars pata de mula ("mule foot") and zopilote ("vulture"), the latter, unfortunately, without the flowers needed for a complete herbarium specimen voucher. Without luck thus far, we have continued to search for mano larga ("long hand") and chino ("curly"). Indeed, of the nine cultivars described by Pérez in the nineteenth century, we now lack good surviving examples only for these two. We continue to search for two other folk varieties, mano anchaque and cucharo, which may or may not be synonyms for already described cultivars. In all of these cases, Trelease's early twentieth century descriptions are unfortunately too incomplete and ambiguous to serve as means to distinguish one cultivar from another, making it difficult to apply the names *Agave palmeri*, *A. pseudotequilana*, or *A. pedrosana* to particular cultivars.

The following descriptions are based on the observations we have made of heirloom cultivars historically used in making tequila, our interpretations of the live plants at Rancho El Indio near Tequila, Jalisco, investigations into the specimens located in the Instituto de Botánica de la Universidad de Guadalajara (IBUG) collection, and the plants around commercial plantations in the Tequila region. We also take into account the descriptions in the literature of Pérez (1887) and Trelease (1920).

⚜ ⚜ ⚜ ⚜ ⚜

Species based on herbarium specimens deposited in the IBUG Jalisco, Mexico

Species	Common Names	Herbarium specimen number
Agave angustifolia ssp. *tequilana* cv. *azul*	azul, mescal azul, mescal de Tequila, chino azul, azulillo, agave tequilero, blue agave	139301 139296 139292 139345 136351
Agave angustifolia ssp. *tequilana* cv. *variegata* (soma-clonal mutant)	azul listado	Without voucher number
Agave angustifolia ssp. *tequilana* cv. *sigüín*	sigüín, criollo sihuín	139298 136350 139394
Agave angustifolia ssp. *rubescens* cv. *pes-mulae*	pie de mula, pata de mula, criollo	Without voucher number
Agave angustifolia cv. *gentryii*	moraleño, pico de gorrión	139297 139299 136349
Agave vivipara var. *bermejo*	chino bermejo, bermejo	139293–95 139300
Agave americana cv. *subtilis*	chato, sahuayo	135486-490
Agave angustifolia cv. *zopilote*	zopilote	Without voucher number

Agave angustifolia ssp. *tequilana* cultivar *azul* (Weber 1902) Valenzuela-Zapata & Nabhan *stat. nov.*

Rosettes glaucous, medium bluish to green, surculose, radiately spreading, 1.2–2.0 m tall with thick spherical or ovoidal stems, 3–7 dm tall at maturity; leaves 90–120 (avg. 140) x 8–12 cm, lanceolate, acuminate, firmly fibrous, mostly rigidly outstretched, concave, ascending to horizontal, widest through the middle, narrowed and thickened toward base, generally bluish to green glaucous, sometimes cross-hatched, the margin straight to undulate or repand; teeth generally regular in size and spacing or rarely irregular, diminishing in size toward the base and apex of the leaf; younger leaves mostly 3–7 mm long through mid-blade, the slender cusps curved or flexed from low pyramidal bases, 2–4 mm wide, tinged with a thin yellow line the tooth base, 0.5–2 cm apart, rarely more remote; spine generally short, 1–2 cm long, rarely longer, flattened or openly grooved above, dark brown, the base broad, tinged with a thin yellow horizontal line, decurrent or not; panicle 5–6 m tall, bulbiferous, large and densely branched with 20–28 large diffusely decompound umbels, occurring along the upper third of the stalk, sometimes falling because of its weight; flowers 60–75 mm long on small pedicels, 3–8 mm long bracteolate; ovary 22–38 mm, 7–8 mm broad, cylindric, six-ridged, with unconstricted short neck, slightly tapered at the base; tube 7–10 mm deep, 10–14 mm wide, funnelform, grooved; tepals subequal, pale green and pale yellow, 23–28 mm long, 4–7 mm wide, linear, erect but withering quickly in anthesis, turning brownish and dry; filaments 45–52 mm long, entirely marbled with purple, bent inwardly against pistil, marbled with purple, inserted and turning at two heights 7 and 5 mm above base of tube; anthers 22–25 mm long slightly marbled in purple; fruits 23–35 mm wide, 38–57 mm broad, capsule ovate, slightly cuspidate, woody, sometimes lacking inner peduncles; seeds often sterile, 7–9 x 5–8 mm, shiny black.

This is the only agave permitted by Mexican law to be used for making tequila. This single cultivar, azul, is cultivated in western Mexico over tens of thousands of hectares over a wide elevation range (100–2,000 m). The shape of the plants is more oval at lower humid elevations (less than 1,600 m), and more spherical in higher, cooler areas (greater than 1,600 m). The leaves are more elongated in hot climates and shorter in colder areas. The agricultural management may also have an effect on plant morphology; plants that grow in shady places have long, flexible leaves and small stems (15 cm) with a greenish color. Soils poor in organic matter produce smaller plants with diminutive flowers.

Agave angustifolia Haw. ssp. *tequilana* cultivar/somaclonal mutant *variegata* Valenzuela-Zapata & Nabhan *stat. nov.*

Rosettes medium bluish to bluish green glaucous, surculose, radiately spreading, 1.2–1.5 m tall with thick ovoidal stems, 3–5 dm tall at maturity; leaves 90–120 x 8–10 cm, lanceolate, acuminate, firm fibrous, mostly rigidly outstretched, concave, ascending to horizontal, widest through the middle, narrowed and thickened toward base, generally bluish green glaucous, variably wide, but at least 2 cm wide and lines yellow on outer margins, also margins slightly pink tinged, straight to undulate or repand; teeth generally regular in size and spacing or rarely irregular, mostly 3–7 mm long through mid-blade, the slender cusps curved or flexed from low pyramidal bases 2–4 mm, the tooth bases from

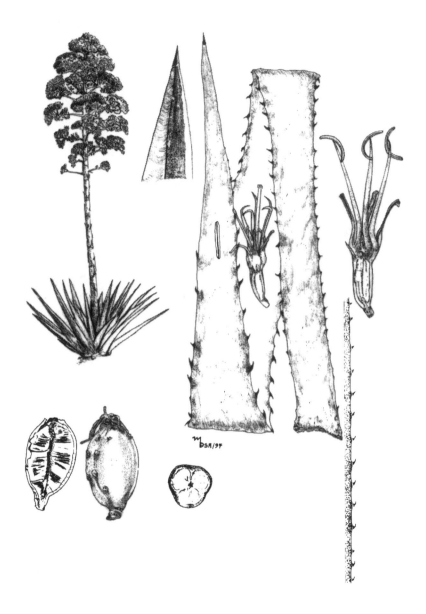

Agave angustifolia ssp. *tequilana* cv. *azul* Valenzuela-Zapata & Nabhan *stat. nov.* Diploid (2n = 60). Common names: *azul, mezcal azul, mezcal de Tequila, chino azul, azulillo, agave tequilero,* and blue agave. (Drawing by Miguel de Santiago Ramírez)

light brown to dark brown, 0.5–2 cm apart, rarely more remote and longer, diminishing in size toward the base and apex of the leaf and on younger leaves; spine generally short, 1–2 cm long, rarely longer, flattened or openly grooved above, dark brown, the base broad with a thin yellow horizontal line, decurrent or not; panicle 5–6 m tall, bulbiferous, large densely branched with 20–28 large diffusely decompound umbels, in the upper third of the stalk; flowers 60–75 mm long on bracteolate pedicels 3–8 mm long; ovary 22–38 mm long, 7–8 mm broad, cylindric, six-ridged, with unconstricted short neck, slightly tapered at the base; tube 7–10 mm deep, 10–14 mm wide, funnelform, grooved; tepals subequal, pale green and yellow, 23–28 mm long, 4–7 mm wide, linear, erect withering quickly in anthesis, turning brownish and dry; filaments 45–52 mm long, somewhat marbled with purple, bent inwardly against pistil, inserted and turning at two heights 7 and 5 mm above base of tube; anthers 22–25 mm long slightly marbled in purple; fruits 23–35 broad, 38 57 mm long, capsule ovate, slightly cuspidate, woody; seeds 5–7 mm equatorial, 7–9 mm polar, shiny black, and with numerous sterile, white seeds.

Although there are not big differences in this variant, which is derived from a single somaclonal mutation, it is proposed here to establish precedence and promote the use of this attractive plant as an ornamental.

Agave angustifolia ssp. *tequilana* cultivar *sigüín* Valenzuela-Zapata & Nabhan *stat. nov.*

Rosettes medium blue greenish to green gray glaucous and colored purple, surculose, radiately spreading, with globose flattened stems, 5–6 dm tall, 4–5 dm wide; mature leaves 100–120 x 8–12 cm, 80–95 leaves, linear to soft lanccolate, strongly acuminate, ascending to horizontal, nearly flat above, smooth, narrowed and thickened toward base, guttered to the apex; spine short, 8–10 mm, broad at base and flattened above, sharp, dark brown; teeth 3–5 mm long, regularly spaced and equal in size, 4–12 mm, slender cusps curved, tinged with a thin yellow line, the tooth bases from light brown to dark brown, diminishing in size toward the base and apex the leaf and younger leaves, margin straight to repand; panicle 3–5 m tall, narrow, with 20–25 short branches in the upper third of the shaft, axis tinged purple, sometimes completely bulbiferous, oval in outline, open, bracteate with triangular bracts that quickly dry purple on the base of the stalk, the flowering umbels diffusive; few flowered, 60–65 mm long, many falling without being fertilized, pale greenish and bright yellow, tepals unequal, 27–30 mm long, 7 mm broad, wilting quickly, long-linear, ovary 27 mm long, 10 mm broad, cylindric, neckless, tapering to pedicel; tube 11–12 mm deep, 14 mm broad, cylindric to globose, narrowly grooved; filaments 48–50 mm long, inserted at 5 mm above the base of the tube, anthers 24–26 mm long, centric or excentric, pistil longer than stamens in post-anthesis, all the parts of the flower are marbled purplish except the body of the ovary and tepals; fruits often entirely absent when solitary plants flowering; when present, broadly ovoid, short stipitate; seeds 5–7 x 7–9 mm, shiny black, sterile seeds numerous.

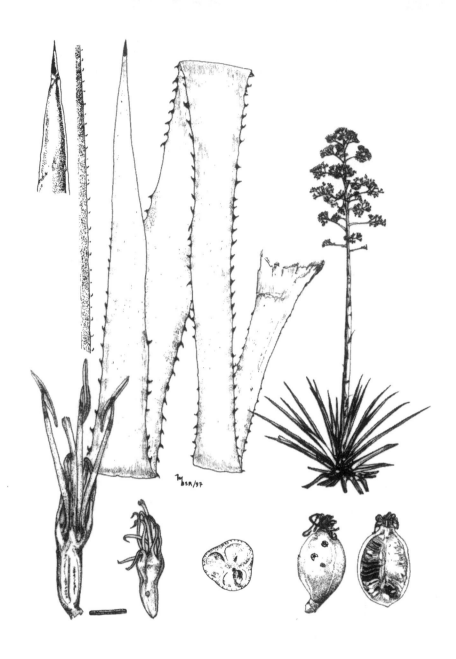

Agave angustifolia ssp. *tequilana* cv. *sigüin* Valenzuela-Zapata & Nabhan *stat. nov.* Diploid 2n = 60. Common names: *sigüin* or *criollo sihuín*. (Drawing by Miguel de Santiago Ramírez)

Sigüín is the cultivar most similar to *Agave angustifolia* ssp. *tequilana* var. *azul.* It can be distinguished from the cultivated variety azul by the narrowed leaf base, reduced lengths of spine and teeth, a light purple tinge to mature plants, and prominently yellow tepals. Sigüín is a plant that flowers early and therefore has a shorter life cycle. Harvested plants of sigüín are difficult to distinguish from azul. Sigüín has broader leaf bases and fewer leaves than azul.

Agave angustifolia ssp. *rubescens* (Gentry) cultivar/var. *pes-mulae* (Trel., 1909) Valenzuela-Zapata & Nabhan *stat. nov.*

Rosettes small, sparsely surculose, symmetrical, radiately spreading, with globose stems, 4–6 dm tall, 3–5 dm wide; mature leaves 70–90 x 4–6 cm, linear straight, mostly acuminate, unequal, ascending to horizontal, nearly flat above, guttered in the apex, blue greenish to gray glaucous, smooth, abruptly narrowed toward base; spine short, 10–12 mm, broad at base and flattened above, dark brown; teeth 2–4 mm long, regular in size and spacing, 8–12 mm, slender cusps curved, broken and remote in the apex, diminishing in size toward the base and apex of the leaf and younger leaves, a thin yellow line tinging the tooth bases from light brown to dark brown, the margin straight; panicle 2–3 m tall, narrow, with 10–20 short branches in upper third or quarter of the shaft, bulbiferous, oval shape, open, bracteate with triangular bracts drying quickly, the flowering umbels small; flowers 60–65 mm long, greenish, few in each of the umbels, tepals unequal, 22–24 mm long, 5 mm broad, wilting quickly, long linear, ovary small 25–27 mm long, 9–10 mm broad, cylindric fusiform, neckless, tapering to pedicel; tube 15–18 mm deep, 12 mm broad, funnelform to cylindric, narrowly grooved, thick-walled below filaments; filaments 45–50 mm long, inserted at wide angle 13–16 mm above the base of the tube, in the last third of the top, anthers 21–31 mm long, centric or excentric, pistil over-reaching stamens in post-anthesis, all the parts of the flower are marble-tipped with purplish except for the body of the ovary and tepals; capsules broadly ovoid, short stipitate; seeds 5–7 x 7–9 mm, shiny black, numerous white sterile seeds.

This plant is very different from the rest of the agaves used for tequila, because of its small size and floral characteristics, including the big tube, the insertion of filaments, and the shape and color of the blossoms. The size of its leaves suggests that the cultivar pata de mula is very close to *Agave angustifolia* var. *rubescens* (Gentry), although *A. angustifolia* var. *rubescens* is a small wild plant. The cultivar name means that the pruned-back plant is similar to a mule's track.

Agave angustifolia cultivar *gentryii* Valenzuela-Zapata & Nabhan *stat. nov.*

Rosettes medium bluish glaucous to gray glaucous, surculose, radiately spreading, 1.2–1.4 m tall with ovoidal stems, 7–9 dm tall inclined, 4.5–5.0 dm broad at maturity; leaves 150–200 (avg. 180) drying on the oldest third of the trunk, 95–110 x 7–10 cm, linear-lanceolate, firmly fibrous, mostly rigidly outstretched, concave, ascending to horizontal, slightly valleculate, widest near the middle, narrowed toward base, generally bluish glaucous to gray glaucous, cross-zoned, the margin straight to undulate or repand; teeth regular in size and spacing, mostly 1–3 mm long through mid-blade, the slender cusps curved from low pyramidal bases 2–3 mm, light brown to dark brown, 1.0–2.0 cm apart, rarely longer, diminishing in size toward the base and apex of the leaf and on younger leaves, remote to absent in the first 10 cm of the apex; spine generally short, 0.7–1.0 cm long, flattened or slightly grooved above, curved below, the base broad with a thin yellow horizontal line, dark brown, not decurrent; panicle 4–8 m tall, bracts chartaceous, 13–20 cm long, branches at 45 degrees to the axis, bulbiferous often in the lowest half of the stalk, branched with 25–35, with compacted, densely globose umbels, narrowly oblong, distributed in upper half of the stalk, sometimes falling because of its heavy weight; flowers 68–79 mm long, light green bluish and pale yellow not marbled, small bracteolate, pedicels 3–5 mm long; ovary 34–41 mm, 7–13 mm broad, cylindric, neckless; tube big, 17–21 mm deep, 10–14 mm wide, straight-funnelform, narrowly grooved toward the ovary, constricted above; tepals subequal, green bluish and pale yellow, 26–30 mm long, 8–10 mm wide, linear, erect but withering quickly in anthesis, turning brownish and dry; filaments light green, 43–61 mm long, bent inward against light green pistil, inserted subequally 13 and 17 mm above base of tube; anthers 20–29 mm long; fruits 20–31.5 mm equatorial, 54–67 mm polar, fusiform and long ovoid, woody; seeds 6.5 x 10.0 mm, shiny black with numerous white sterile seeds.

High saponin content and low alcohol production of alcohol are among the diagnostic characteristics of this cultivar and the reasons that it became marginal in the tequila industry. Its small, numerous leaves have strong fibers that are remarkably durable in textiles and cordage compared to those of other cultivars grown for fiber. It also has an inflorescence with relatively dense umbels for a species in the Rigidae group, which is characterized by pale greenish flowers having long floral tubes. We propose it as a new taxon, *Agave angustifolia* cv. *gentryii*, dedicated to Dr. Howard Scott Gentry, in honor of his astute, diligent, and creative efforts over fifty years in making sense of agaves.

Agave vivipara (*A. cantala* Roxb. 1814) var. *bermejo* Valenzuela-Zapata & Nabhan *stat. nov.*

Rosettes huge, sparsely surculose, radiately spreading, 2.0–2.20 m tall before flowering, with ovoidal big stems, 6–9 dm tall, 4.8–6.0 dm broad; leaves 120–160, reflexed at maturity, 100–170 x 12–16 cm, linear-lanceolate, long acuminate, firm fibrous, mostly rigidly outstretched, concave, ascending to horizontal, widest near the middle, thickened and flattened toward base, guttered from the middle to the apex, bright green to bluish-green glaucous, cross-hatched, the margin straight to undulate or repand, surface smooth; teeth regular in size and spacing

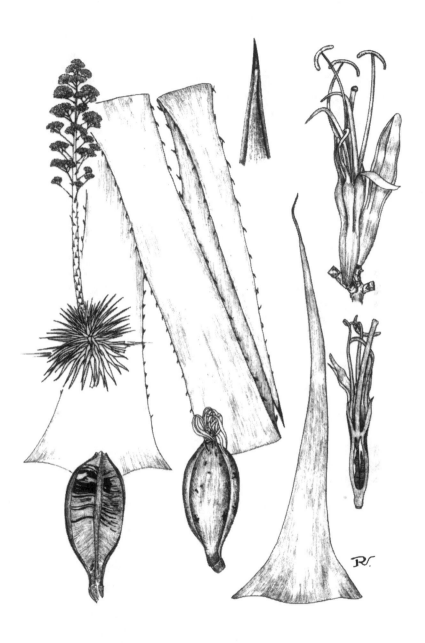

Agave angustifolia cv. *gentryii* Valenzuela-Zapata & Nabhan *stat. nov.*
Common names: *moraleño* or *pico de gorrión*. (Drawing by María del
Refugio Vázquez Velasco)

or rarely irregular, mostly 3–8 mm long through mid-blade, 1.0–2.5 cm apart, low pyramidal bases 2–4 mm, deltoids, slender cusps curved to straight, flexed, tooth bases tinged with a thin yellow line, light reddish brown to reddish dark brown, often absent in the apex, diminishing in size toward the base and apex of the leaf; spine generally short, 0.5–1.5 cm long, rarely longer, conical, a thin yellow line tinging the base, not decurrent, slightly flattened above; panicle 6–8 m tall, scarcely bulbiferous, open, large branched, diffuse umbels, peduncles slender, horizontal to slightly curved, pyramidal, slightly ovoidal in outline, 20–40 large umbels, in the upper half to two-thirds of stalk, bracts chartaceous triangular, 8–16 cm near the bottom, branch bracts adherent and broken; green flowers 60–75 mm long on minutely bracteolate pedicels, slender; ovary 22–38 mm, 10–12 mm broad, neckless, fusiform, cylindrical, shortly curved and larger toward the base; tube 7–14 mm deep, 10–14 mm wide, 8–9 mm broad in the base, funnelform, narrowly grooved; tepals subequal, yellow up to the middle, apex roseate, 22–27 x 8–11 mm, linear, withering quickly in anthesis, turning brownish and dry, erect or reflexed in anthesis, fetid odor, caducous in the first umbels; pistil over-reaching filaments in anthesis, velvety stigma marbled with reddish-rose; filaments 35–45 mm long, marbled in purple only from the middle to the apex, inserted and turning at heights of 8–12 mm above the base of the tube; anthers 15–24 mm long, irregular in size, yellow; fruits 23–35 broad, 38–57 mm long, capsule ovoidal, slightly cuspidate, wooded walls; seeds 5 x 7 mm, shiny black, more sterile seeds than fertile.

Recently Smith and Steyn (1999) argued on the basis of their historic interpretations of literature, plants generally recognized by the name of *Agave angustifolia* should correctly be attributed to *A. vivipara*. However, a more recent note (Grayum, Hammel, and Zamora 1999) reports that a subsequent, more detailed examination of the lectotype illustration of *A. vivipara* corroborated Gentry's (1982) suspicion that the name correctly applies to *A. cantala*, another species well known in cultivation.

Considering the very different characteristics of *A. cantala*, we are confident that this cultivated tequila-producing agave belongs here. We are proposing it as the variety bermejo of *A. vivipara*, a taxon that has historic priority over *A. cantala*. The distinctive characteristics of this plant, known as chino bermejo, are its large size and deep green color. Its fetid blossoms and the loss of leaf turgidity during flowering are reminiscent of those of sisal cultivars *(A. sisalana)*. It is difficult to find this cultivar in agave azul plantations today, but the old mescaleros recall harvesting plants weighing 150 kg or more, when it was more common.

Agave americana cultivar *subtilis* (*A. subtilis* Trel. 1920) Valenzuela-Zapata & Nabhan *stat. nov.*

Rosettes 1.70–2.0 m tall, short stemmed, 7–10 dm broad, suckering, in open big rosettes, symmetrical with 80–100 leaves at maturity; leaves rigid linear-patulous, 150–200 x 15–16.5 cm broad, long acuminate, very broad at the base, cross

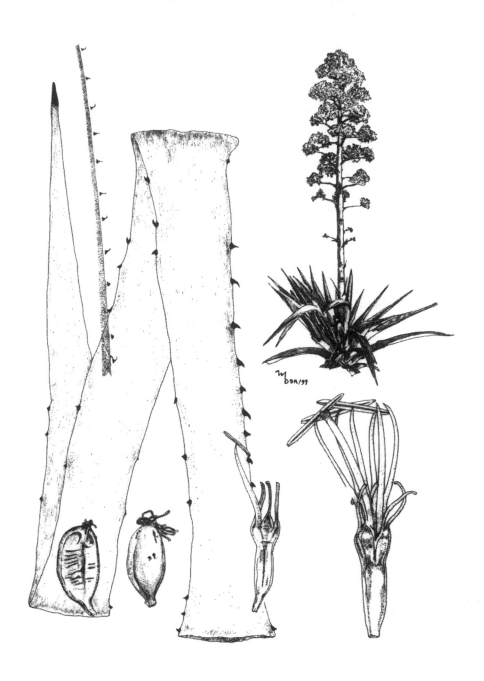

Agave vivipara (*A. cantala* Roxb. 1814) var. *bermejo* Valenzuela-Zapata & Nabhan *stat. nov.* Common names: *chino bermejo* or *bermejo*. (Drawing by Miguel de Santiago Ramírez)

zoned, flat to guttering upward, valleculate, light green to bluish-gray glaucous, margin straight to repand; teeth 10–15 mm long, 0.5–3.0 cm apart, smaller and more closely spaced toward the base, with broad pyramidal bases, 7–15 mm wide, slender cusps not centered near the base, irregularly curved to sigmoidal to straight, tinged light to dark brown, with a yellow thin line on the base; spine 2–2.5 cm, subulate to acicular, open grooved above, sharp, decurrent, shiny dark brown to blackish; inflorescence 6–10 m; paniculate on upper third to half of shaft, bracts 25–35 in number at the bottom, 10–20 cm, pyramidal-ovoid in outline, with small compact umbels, the peduncle with chartaceous erect bracts; pedicels 8–10 mm; flowers 8–10 cm thick and fleshy, light green and yellow; ovary 30–42 x (8–15 mm, fusiform, tapered to slightly curve at the base; tube globose, 17–21 mm long, 18–20 mm broad, constricted at apex; tepals 32–42 mm long, pale yellow to yellow, scarcely involute, withering quickly in anthesis, erect and reflexed, 10–12 mm broad, neck 6–10 mm, grooved; filaments 55–85 cm, marbled purplish-brownish, inserted above the tube 13–17 mm, curved and thickened at the base, thin flattened in the apex; anthers 28–41 mm, completely marbled purplish-brownish, excentric; pistil much thicker than filaments, purplish-brownish along tips; fruits numerous, 25–34 mm wide, 48–60 mm broad, ovoidal, short stipitate; seeds bright black, 6–8 mm wide x 8.5–10 mm long.

This cultivar is commonly named "chato" or "sahuayo." The latter is for Sahuayo, Michoacán, where this plant has been cultivated to make mescal since before written history. It was described as *Agave subtilis* for its small stem by Trelease (1920). We propose that it is a variant of *A. americana,* one widely distributed and used by the ancient Aztecs, and their relatives of Mesoamerica. This variant is easily distinguished from other tequila-producing agaves by its size, wide leaves, and heavier spines. It was often rejected by the tequila mills because the toughness of its fibers made it unsuitable for sugar extraction. Its rigid, linear, and spoon-shaped leaves are not very typical of the *A. americana,* but its overall characteristics are consistent with this species. Because of its floral structure, the tubes of *A. subtilis* hold a large amount of nectar.

Agave angustifolia cultivar *zopilote*

Plants medium size, open rosettes 1.30 x 1.50 m, shorter stemmed, scarcely surculose, radiately spreading; leaves 10–15 dm x 8–10 cm, unequal younger leaves, soft, linear, strongly acuminate, valleculate, guttered, thinning toward the apex, easily broken, narrowed and thickened toward fleshy base, bright green to green glaucous, margin straight to undulate, reddish tinged during cold season; teeth irregular in size and spacing, 5–30 mm apart, tips slender flexuous, slightly recurved to totally repand, bases pyramidal 2–4 mm, tinged with a thin yellow line, light to dark brown with aging; spine 2–2.5 cm broad conical, shallowly grooved above, sides decurrent, sharp, dark brown.

This plant has affinities with the diverse *Agave angustifolia* complex, but because we still lack reproductive specimens, we cannot confirm exactly where its placement should be. This variant has extremely slow growth rates, with its

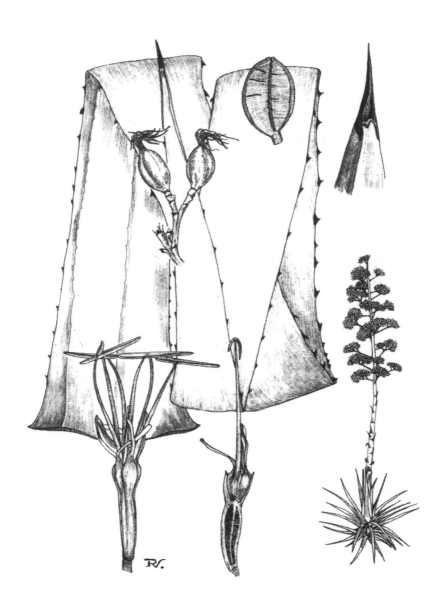

Agave americana cv. *subtilis* (*A. subtilis* Trel. 1909) Valenzuela-Zapata &
Nabhan *stat. nov.* Common names: *chato* or *sahuayo*. (Drawing by María
del Refugio Vázquez Velasco)

few leaves unfolding and maturing over more than a decade. Its small armature and thickened fleshy leaf bases are indicators of its ripening and readiness for harvest. It is called "zopilote" ("vulture") by most mescaleros, but is also referred to as *"zopolochino"* by others.

Literature Cited

↟ ↟ ↟

Alfaro, A. 1994. El agave simbólico. El tequila y sus signos: elogio del Hidalgo campirano. El tequila: Arte tradicional de México. *Artes de México* 27:11.

Álvarez de Zayas, A. 1995. Los agaves de las Antillas. *Boletín de la Sociedad Botánica de México* 57:37–48.

Arita, H. T., and C. Martinez del Rio. 1988. *La interacción flor-murciélago.* Mexico City: Monografía del Instituto de Biologia de la UNAM.

Arita, H. T., and D. E. Wilson. 1989. Long-nosed bats and agaves: the tequila connection. *Bats* 3:4–6.

Bahre, C. J., and D. E. Bradbury. 1980. Manufacture of mescal in Sonora, Mexico. *Economic Botany* 34(4):391–400.

Barjau, L. 1997. *Tequila.* Mexico City: Editorial Cal y Arena.

Borewell, T., 1995. Bootlegging on a desert mountain: the political ecology of agave (*Agave* spp.) demographic change in the Sonora River Valley, Sonora, Mexico. *Human Ecology* 23(3):407–32.

Bruman, H. J. 1935. The Asiatic origin of the Huichol still. *Geographical Review* 34:418–27.

Bye, R. A. 1979. An 1878 ethnobotanical collection from San Luis Potosí: Dr. Edward Palmer's first major Mexican collection. *Economic Botany* 33(2):135–62.

————. 1993. The role of humans in the diversification of plants in Mexico. In *Biological Diversity in Mexico,* edited by T. P. Ramamoorthy et al. Oxford University Press.

Bye, R. A., D. Burgess, and A. B. Tryan. 1975. Ethnobotany of the western Tarahumara of Chihuahua. I. Notes on the genus *Agave. Botanical Museum Leaflets* 24:85–112.

Cabrera, L. 1994. *Diccionario de Aztequismos.* México City, D.F.: Colofón.

Castetter, E. F., W. H. Bell, and A. R. Grove. 1938. The early utilization and distribution of *Agave* in the American Southwest. *University of New Mexico Bulletin* 335.

CENTENAL. 1981. Cartas geologicas y de suelo para Tequila, Jalisco. México City, D.F.: CENTENAL, Mexican government printing office.

Colunga García-Marín, P., and F. May-Pat. 1997. Morphological variation of henequén (*Agave fourcroydes*, Agavaceae) germplasm and its wild ancestor (*A. angustifolia*) under uniform growth conditions: diversity and domestication. *American Journal of Botany* 84(11):1449–65.

De Orellana, M. 1994. El agave tenaz. Microhistoria del tequila: el caso Cuervo. El tequila: Arte tradicional de México. *Artes de México* 27:33.

Eguiarte, L. E., M. R. Duvall, G. H. Learn, Jr., and M. T. Clegg. 1997. Filogenia molecular de las familias Agavaceae y Nolinaceae: análisis basados en la secuencia del gen del cloroplasto *rbc*L. Primer Simposio Internaciónal Sobre Agavaceae. UNAM Jardin Botanico Memorias: 14.

Felger, R. S., and M. B. Moser. 1985. *People of the desert and sea: Ethnobotany of the Seri Indians.* Tucson: University of Arizona Press.

Fish, S. K., P. R. Fish, C. Miksicek, and J. Madson. 1985. Prehistoric agave cultivation in southern Arizona. *Desert Plants* 7(2):107–12.

Fitzpatrick, E. A. 1984. *Suelos: Su formación, clasificación y distribución.* Mexico City, D.F.: Compania Editorial Continental.

Forster, P. L. 1992. New varietal combinations in *Agave vivipara* (Agavaceae). *Brittonia* 44(1):74–75.

Franco-Martínez, I. S. 1995. Conservación *in-situ* y *ex-situ* de las agaváceas y noliáceas mexicanas. *Boletín de la Sociedad Botánica de México.* 57:27–36.

Galindo, O. 1999. De Jalisco es el tequila. *El Vino y Otras Delicias* 1(2):30–40.

García-Mendoza, A. 1998. *Con sabor a maguey.* México City, D.F.: Jardin Botanico de la UNAM.

García-Mendoza, A., and R. Galván-Villanueva. 1995. Riquezas de la familias Agavaceae y Nolinaceae en México. *Boletín Sociedad Botánica, México* 56:7–24.

Garibay, K. S. 1988. Enraizamiento de hijuelos en viveros de "Agave azul tequilero" *Agave tequilana* Weber utilizando hormonas. Tesis de Licenciatura, Facultad de Agronomía, Universidad de Guadalajara.

Gentry, H. S. 1972. The agave family in Sonora. USDA *Agricultural Handbook* 399.

————. 1975. The man-agave symbiosis. *Saguaroland Bulletin* 29(7):80–84.

————. 1982. *Agaves of continental North America.* Tucson: University of Arizona Press.

Gonçalves de Lima, O. 1978. *El maguey y el pulque en los códices Mexicanos.* México City, D.F.: Fondo de Cultura Económica.

————. 1990. Pulque, balché, y pajauaru en la etnobiología de las bebidas y de los alimentos fermentados. Mexico City, D.F.: Fondo de Cultura Económica.

Gould, F. 1986. Simulation models for predicting durability of insect-resistant germplasm: Hessian fly (Diptera: Cecidomyiidae) resistant winter wheat. *Environmental Entomology* 15:11–23.

Granados, S. D. 1985. Etnobotánica de los agaves de las zonas áridas y semiáridas.

Biología y aprovechamiento integral del henequén y otros agaves. Centro de Investigación Científica Yucatán, A.C. 127–35.

Grayum, M. H., B. E. Hammel, and N. Zamora, eds. 1999. *Cutting Edge* [serial on-line] 6(4). Available at: http://www.mobot.org/MOBOT/research/edge/oct99/oct99lit.html.

Heacox, K. 1989. Fatal attraction? *International Wildlife* 19(3):39–43.

Henestrosa, A. 1997. *Mezcal, elixir de larga vida.* Oaxaca City: DISTRAGSA.

Hernandez-Xolocotzi, E. 1993. Aspects of plant domestication in México: A personal view. In *Biological diversity in Mexico: Origins and distribution*, edited by T. P. Ramamoorthy et al. Oxford University Press.

Heyden, D. 1983. *Mitología y simbolismo de la flora en el México prehispánico.* México: Universidad Nacional Autónoma de México.

Hodgson, W., G. P. Nabhan, and L. Ecker. 1989. Conserving rediscovered agave cultivars. *Agave* 3:9–11.

Hutson, L. 1995. *Tequila! Cooking with the spirit of Mexico.* San Francisco: Ten Speed Press.

Instituto Nacional Estadistica Geografica e Informativa (INEGI). 1997. *El Agave tequilero en el estado de Jalisco.* Mexico City, D.F.: INEGI.

Kulander, C. 1992. *West México: From sea to sierra.* Ramona, California: La Paz Publishing.

León-Portilla, M. 1995. *Toltecayotl: Aspectos de la cultura Nahuatl.* 5th ed. Mexico City, D.F.: Editorial Fondo de Cultura Económica.

Lezama, M. M. 1975. El maguey. *El Campo: Revista Mensual Agrícola y Ganadera.* 16.

Lowry, M. 1971. *Under the volcano.* New York: Plume.

Luna-Zamora, R. 1991. *La historia del tequila, de sus regiones y sus hombres.* México City, D.F.: CONACULTA.

Martínez-Limón, E. 1998. *Tequila: Tradición y destino.* México City, D.F.: Revimundo.

Muriá, J. M. 1990. El tequila. *Boceto histórico de una industria, Cuadernos de difusión científica.* Guadalajara, México: Universidad de Guadalajara. 85.

Muriá, J. M., and R. Sanchez. 1996. *Una bebida llamada tequila.* Guadalajara, Mexico: Editorial Agata.

Nabhan, G. P. 1985. Drinking away the centuries. In *Gathering the desert*, by G. P. Nabhan and P. Mirocha. Tucson: University of Arizona Press.

———. 1994. Finding the hidden garden. In *Desert legends*, by G. P. Nabhan and M. Klett. New York: Henry Holt.

———. 1997. Tequila hangovers and the mescal monoculture blues. In *Cultures of Habitat.* Washington, D.C.: Counterpoint Press.

Nabhan, G. P., and T. Fleming. 1993. The conservation of New World mutualisms. *Conservation Biology* 7(3):457–59.

Nelson, S. C., G. P. Nabhan, and R. H. Robichaux. 1991. Effects of water, nitrogen and competition on growth, yield and yield components of field-grown tepary bean. *Experimental Agriculture* 27:211–19.

Nobel, P. S. 1988. *Environmental biology of agaves and cacti.* Cambridge: Cambridge University Press.

—————. 1994. *Remarkable agaves and cacti.* New York: Oxford University Press.

Nobel P. S., and E. Quero. 1986. Environmental productivity indices for a Chihuahuan desert CAM plant, *Agave lechugilla. Ecological Society of America* 1.

Nobel, P. S., and A. G. Valenzuela-Zapata. 1987. Environmental responses and productivity of the CAM plant, *Agave tequilana* W. *Agricultural Meteorology* 39:319–34.

Norma de denominación de origen del tequila. 1978. *Diario Oficial de la Federación,* 5 November. 7–12.

—————. 1994. *Diario Oficial de la Federación,* 31 May. 24–28.

Osawa, T. 1979. El mezcal: Ideas sobre su mejoramiento y técnicas de control. Unpublished manuscript.

Parsons, J. R., and M. H. Parsons. 1990. *Maguey utilization in highland central Mexico: An archaeological ethnography.* Ann Arbor: Museum of Anthropology, University of Michigan.

Pérez, L. 1887. Estudio sobre el agave llamado mezcal. *Boletín de la Sociedad Agrícola Mexicana, Mexico* (11):132–36.

Plascencia-Adame, O. R. 1985. Evaluación técnica económica sobre el cultivo del agave. Bachelor's thesis, Facultad de Agricultura, Universidad de Guadalajara, Zapopan, Jalisco.

Plascencia-Adame, O. R., and J. Tapia, 1990. *El agave azul de las mieles al tequila.* Mexico City, D.F.: Instituto Francés de América Latina.

Promotora Regional del Agave, S. de R.L. de C.V. 1985. Establecimiento y manejo del agave tequilero. Privately distributed brochure, Guadalajara, Mexico.

Ramirez-Rancano, M. 1999. Abundancia de alcohol y tabaco en el México contemporáneo. *Ciencia y Desarrollo* 25(145):40–47.

Rivera, C. 1983. Estudio citogenetico y fitogeografico de *Agave* aff. *tequilana* Weber y *A. karwinskii* Zucc. en los valles de Tehuacan, Puebla, y centrales de Oaxaca. Tesis de Licenciatura, ENEP/IZTACALA, UNAM, México City, D.F.

Romero, L. 1998. El agave azul afectado por plagas y bacterias. *Ciencia y Desarollo* 143:4–7.

Rosen, M. D. 1995. Monsanto in Mexico's agave fields. *Monsanto Magazine* 2:20–23.

Sánchez-Armenta, F. 1991. Comparación de metodologías de micropropagación de *Agave tequilana* Weber. Professional thesis, Facultad de Agronomia, Universidad de Guadalajara, Zapopoan, Jalisco.

Sánchez-Lacy, A. R. 1998. *Guia del tequila.* México City, D.F.: Artes de Mexico.

Secretaria de Agricultura y Recursos Hidraulicos. 1974. Programa para establecer y rehabilitar plantaciones de *Agave.* Mexico City, D.F.: Fideicomiso en Nacional Financiera, Gobierno Federal y Naciones Unidas.

Secretaria de Comercio y Fomento Industrial (SECOFI). 1994. Resolución de ortoga la protección a la denominación del origen mezcal. *Diario Oficial de la Federación.* 28 November. 27–30.

Serna, E. 1995. El charro cantor. In *Mitos Mexicanos*, edited by E. Florescano. Mexico City, D.F.: Editorial Aguilar Nuevo Siglo.

Sheridan, T. E. 1988. *Where the dove calls*. Tucson: University of Arizona Press.

Smith, G. F., and E.M.A. Steyn. 1999. *Agave vivipara:* the correct name for *Agave angustifolia*. *Bothalia* 29:100.

Sobarzo, H. 1991. *Vocabulario Sonorense*. Hermosillo: State of Sonora/Instituto Cultural Sonorense.

Trelease, W. 1920. *Agave*. In *Trees and shrubs of Mexico*, by P. C. Standley. Washington, D.C.: GPO.

Valenzuela-Zapata, A. G. 1985. The tequila industry in Jalisco, México. *Desert Plants* 2:65–70.

————. 1987. La poda en el agave tequilero (*Agave tequilana* Weber), y su influencia en la productividad. Tesis de Licenciatura, Universidad de Guadalajara, Facultad de Agronomía, Guadalajara, Mexico.

————. 1991. La jima. *Boletín Técnico Agrícola* (Guadalajara, México: Tequila Sauza S. A. De C.V.) Nos. 0–6.

————. 1992. Fertilización en plantas jóvenes de agave tequilero (*Agave tequilana* Weber, variedad azul). Tesis de Maestra en Ciencias, Escuela de Graduados, Universidad de Guadalajara, Guadalajara, Mexico.

————. 1995. La agroindustria del agave tequilero *Agave tequilana* Weber. *Boletín de la Sociedad de Botánica de México* 55:15–25.

————. 1994. *El agave tequilero: Su cultivo e industria*. Guadalajara, Mexico: Monsanto.

————. 1997. *El agave tequilero: Su cultivo e industria*. Guadalajara, Mexico: Monsanto.

Vigueras-Guzmán, A. L. 1993. Inventario preliminar de los agaves en Jalisco y algunos datos sobre su distribución. *Boletín de la Sociedad Jalisciense de Cactalogia* 5(3):49–54.

Villalvazo-Rodriguez, A. S. 1986. El cultivo del mezcal (*Agave tequilana* Weber) en la región de Tequila, Jalisco. Tesis de Licenciatura, Universidad de Chapingo, Texcoco, Mexico.

Wallis, M., and T. Moore. 1982. In the land of tequila. *American West Magazine* September/October:41–49.

Walton, N. K. 1977. The evolution and localization of mezcal and tequila in Mexico. *Review of the Geographical Institute of Panamerican Geographical History* 85: 113–32.

Wijnands, D. O. 1983. *The botany of the commelins*. Rotterdam: Balkema.

About the Authors

✦ ✦ ✦

Ana Guadalupe Valenzuela-Zapata is recognized in Mexico and the United States as the foremost botanical and horticultural expert on agaves used in the tequila industry. A professor at the Universidad de Guadalajara, and one of the few women field scientists in a male-dominated industry, she is author of the Spanish language book, *El Agave Tequilero,* and numerous scientific articles on the blue agave. She has received bachelor's and master's of science degrees from the Universidad de Guadalajara, and is currently involved in research on advancing the sustainability of agave production in a Ph.D. program at the Universidad Autonoma de Nuevo Leon.

Gary Paul Nabhan has done field research on agave conservation and use for a quarter century in the United States and Mexico. He is a recipient of a MacArthur "Genius Award" Fellowship and a Lifetime Achievement Award from the Society for Conservation Biology. Nabhan is author or coauthor of sixteen books, three of which have received national or international awards. He is Director of the Center for Sustainable Environments at Northern Arizona University.